A PRIMER FOR BEGINNING PSYCHOTHERAPY

Second Edition

A PRIMER FOR BEGINNING PSYCHOTHERAPY

Second Edition

William N. Goldstein, M.D.
Baltimore-Washington Institute for Psychoanalysis
Georgetown University Medical Center

USA	Publishing Office:	BRUNNER-ROUTLEDGE
		A member of the Taylor & Francis
		325 Chestnut Street
		Philadelphia, PA 19106
		Tel: (215) 625-8900
		Fax: (215) 625-2940

**WM
420
G6252p
2001**

	Distribution Center:	BRUNNER-ROUTLEDGE
		A member of the Taylor & Francis
		7625 Empire Drive
		Florence, KY 41042
		Tel: 1 (800) 634-7064
		Fax: 1 (800) 248-4724

UK		BRUNNER-ROUTLEDGE
		A member of the Taylor & Francis Group
		27 Church Road
		Hove
		E. Sussex, BN3 2FA
		Tel.: +44 (0) 1273 207411
		Fax: +44 (0) 1273 205612

A PRIMER FOR BEGINNING PSYCHOTHERAPY, SECOND EDITION

1 2 3 4 5 6 7 8 9 0

Printed by George H. Buchanan, Philadelphia, PA, 2001.

A CIP catalog record for this book is available from the British Library.
∞ The paper in this publication meets the requirements of the ANSI Standard Z39.48-1984 (Permanence of Paper).

Library of Congress Cataloging-in-Publication Data
Goldstein, William N.
    A primer for beginning psychotherapy / William N. Goldstein.—2nd ed.
      p. cm.
    Includes bibliographical references and index.
    ISBN 1-58391-074-3 (alk. paper)
    1. Psychotherapy. I. Title.

    RC480.5 G615 2001
    616.89'14—dc21

                          00-046675

ISBN: 1-58391-074-3 (paper)

CONTENTS

PREFACE

The second edition of the primer provides several useful additions. First and foremost of these is a chapter on contemporary schools of thought. Although once preeminent amongst psychotherapies with psychodynamic orientations, ego psychology is now only one of several highly influential schools of thought. Other competing models include self psychology, intersubjectivity, object relations theory, social constructionism, and the relational school. The chapter on contemporary schools offers succinct summaries of these varying models, comparing and contrasting each. The primer focuses mainly on clinical and practical matters. Thus, although it emphasizes an ego psychological approach, it can be equally useful to therapists using these other competing models.

The second edition also presents a number of new practical topics. These include discussions regarding the frequency of sessions, the spacing of sessions, answering questions, accepting gifts, self disclosures, and enactments. Finally, an appendix on ego functions has been added. Designed especially for therapists unfamiliar with this way of thinking, the appendix should be particularly useful with regard to classifying patients into one of the four large diagnostic groupings.

PREFACE
TO THE FIRST EDITION

Designed especially for students and mental health professionals at the early stages of their careers, this primer provides a practical guide for doing psychotherapy. Short and concise, it addresses virtually all questions that a neophyte therapist might have. A major goal is to present the basics in a clear and succinct way, with special emphasis on techniques and clinical example.

The primer begins by looking at the patients: who they are and why they come for psychotherapy. A classification dividing all patients into one of four large groupings—normal–neurotic, narcissistic, borderline, and psychotic—is elaborated. This classification is especially useful, each large grouping being associated with its own therapeutic strategies, approaches, and techniques. Throughout the book, there is comparison and contrast regarding each of the four groupings.

The primer next addresses the therapists: who they are, what attracts them to the field, and inherent problems with which they will have to deal. The personal characteristics, experiences, and training deemed most useful for these individuals are addressed, in addition to the issues of sex, ethnic group, and specialization.

An overview of psychotherapy is then presented. The different types of psychotherapy are conceptualized on a continuum with the most insight-oriented and exploratory types at one end and the most supportive types at the other. Five types of psychotherapy along this continuum are described: psychoanalysis, analytically oriented psychotherapy, modified analytically oriented psychotherapy, dynamically oriented psychotherapy, and supportive psychotherapy. Cognitive therapy is also discussed. Emphasis is on what kinds of patients do best with each of the different therapies.

The next four chapters address questions related to getting started. A chapter on the larger issues regarding psychotherapy focuses on the stability of the therapeutic environment, the neutrality and flexibility of the therapist, countertransference, empathy, the activity of the therapist, and the mechanism of change in psychotherapy. A chapter on arrangements discusses scheduling, payments, missed appointments, guidelines for the patient, contracts, and smoking and food in the sessions. A separate chapter provides instruction about how to arrange the office, while one on the initial interview highlights interactions between patient and therapist at this beginning stage of treatment.

The remainder of the book focuses on the nitty-gritty of psychotherapy. Here techniques and interventions are spelled out in detail, amply illustrated by clinical vignettes. Chapters on transference and the therapeutic alliance and on the basic strategy provide necessary theoretical background. A chapter on therapeutic interventions describes the various types of interventions, the selection of interventions, and the manner and style of interventions. This chapter also discusses affirmative interpretations, preparatory comments, feedback from the patient, lateness, missed appointments, and the 5-minute warning.

A chapter on interventions regarding anxiety and defense details techniques using this conceptual framework, providing applications to all four large groupings. A chapter on special issues and problems addresses primitive defenses, projective identification, severe acting out, the suicidal patient, difficulties with reality testing, dreams, and medication. The primer ends with a chapter discussing phases, trends, and termination.

The Patients

1. Who Are the Patients?

Patients include anybody and everybody. They come from all walks of life, all socioeconomic states, and all ethnic groups. They present with unending variation in regard to character traits, personalities, and behavior. What they have in common is that they suffer from problems that interfere with their attaining their life goals, maximizing their potentials, and leading basically contented lives. Their problems stem from conflicts that are at least partially outside of their awarenesses. These problems vary in intensity and present either as symptoms or as personality traits and patterns. Often the problems are overtly bothersome to the patients. At other times, although they do not cause discomfort, they interfere with the patients' lives in ways that have become apparent to them.

2. Can Patients Be Conveniently Placed into Diagnostic Groups?

Patients can be classified in endless ways. One diagnostic system, particularly useful for psychotherapy, places all patients into one of four large groupings: normal-neurotic, narcissistic, borderline, and psychotic. Each of these groupings can be differentiated by a focus on ego functioning. Although not currently in vogue, a focus on ego functioning is a most effective way of both describing and understanding patients. Although based on psychoanalytic theory, this approach can be thought of as a bridge between descriptive and dynamic thinking in that ego functions can be examined totally descriptively or can be viewed as an aid to dynamic understanding.

Anna Freud (1936) and Hartmann (1939) were among the first to list and describe various functions of the ego. More recently, Beres (1956) and Bellak (1958) enumerated a number of ego functions, including reality testing, sense of reality, adaptation to reality, impulse control and frustration tolerance, object relations, thought processes, defensive functioning, autonomous functions, and the synthetic integrative function. Bellak (1970) and Bellak and Meyers (1975) added several other ego functions: judgment, adaptive regressive in the service of the ego, stimulus barrier, and mastery competence. Of these, I (1985) emphasize the first seven when making the differential diagnosis between the four large groupings. In addition, I focus on interpersonal relations, identity, and stability of affect.

Through an assessment of ego functioning, all individuals can be classified into one of the four large groupings. A diagnosis made in this way can serve as a supraordinate or first-level diagnosis. Later, more specific and secondary diagnoses can be added, providing further descriptive information. If one desires, *Diagnostic and Statistical Manual of Mental Disorders* (*DSM-IV*; American Psychiatric Association, 1994) diagnoses can be used as the secondary diagnosis. One caveat is in order. There will be individuals on the borders between the different groupings, and this can lead to certain ambiguities and uncertainties. Nevertheless, diagnoses made in accordance with the four large groupings are seen as basic with regard to psychotherapeutic approach.

The remainder of the questions in this chapter relate to ego functioning (Goldstein, 1985). If one is not accustomed to a focus on ego functions, reading this chapter might be difficult. To aid with this task, an appendix on ego functions is provided. Some might want to read the more clinical parts of the primer first, then, with the help of the appendix, return to this chapter.

3. What Are the Characteristics of the Normal-Neurotic Grouping?

The hallmark of the normal-neurotic grouping is basically good ego functioning. All ego functions in this grouping are basically intact, with minimal episodic regressions varying from person to person. Thus, the normal-neurotic individual is characterized by intact reality testing, secondary process thinking, good interpersonal relations, good adaptation to reality, good impulse control and frustration tolerance, a stable identity, and affective stability. Defenses are typically mature and neurotic in day-to-day functioning, with neurotic defenses becoming accentuated under stress. There is occasional slippage to immature and borderline defenses, mostly under stress. The preponderance of certain specific neurotic defenses in day-to-day functioning, especially under stress, differentiates one neurotic classification from another. Thus, a "typical" obsessive-compulsive individual tends to use intellectualization, isolation of affect, undoing, reaction formation, and rationalization, whereas a "typical" hysterical person tends to use repression, dramatization, and heightened affect. It should be noted that the hysterical individual referred to here is that of the psychoanalytic literature rather than the *DSM-IV* histrionic personality.

Regarding object relations, the normal-neurotic presents a clearly integrated, cohesive, and stable sense of self and a similarly integrated, cohesive, and stable sense of objects. Others are viewed as complex individuals, clearly having needs and desires of their own. The normal–neurotic typically respects these needs while displaying a certain amount of concern, empathy, and sensitivity. The normal-neurotic thus does not view others as need-fulfilling objects, nor does he or she display identity diffusion. Elaborating on some of the ego functions, interpersonal relations and adaptation to reality may vary somewhat, often in accordance with the pattern of neurotic defenses employed. There can be some slippage in frustration tolerance and impulse control, as well as in affective stability. Rarely are there any problems with reality testing or thought processes.

Although I know many people who function quite well, adapting flexibly and reasonably to the vicissitudes of life, I do not think that I know anyone whom I would call "normal." All people use numerous neurotic defenses and have at least some minimal episodic difficulties with a number of the ego functions. If one had to differentiate between the "so-called" normal and the neurotic, one might emphasize the exaggerated use of certain neurotic defenses with a corresponding decrease in adaptation in the latter group. Because distinctions between the normal and neurotic are both arbitrary and subjective, the normal and neurotic are here classified together to provide the "healthy" grouping in this diagnostic classification.

4. What Are the Characteristics of the Borderline Grouping?

The hallmark of the borderline grouping is a characteristic ego profile consisting of a specific pattern of four relative ego strengths and four underlying ego weaknesses (Goldstein, 1985, 1996). The relative ego strengths are as follows:

1. The relative intactness of reality testing.
2. The relative intactness of thought processes.
3. The relative intactness of interpersonal relations.
4. The relative intactness of the adaptation to reality.

It must be stressed that these four strengths are only relative; they easily break down to various degrees in various situations. Because these four relative strengths stand out superficially, they enable the borderline patient to present a fairly "normal" appearance. These relative strengths, particularly the first two, most clearly differentiate the borderline from the more psychotic individual.

The underlying ego weaknesses are as follows:

1. The combination of poor impulse control and poor frustration tolerance.
2. The proclivity to use primitive ego defenses.
3. The syndrome of identity diffusion.
4. Affective instability.

In contrast to the strengths, which stand out on a superficial level, these weaknesses become clearly apparent only with in-depth understanding. Except during regressed states, a detailed history or a relationship over time is needed for these weaknesses to clearly emerge. Because the weaknesses are beneath the surface and are not detected superficially, they do not detract from the borderline's appearance of normality. These underlying weaknesses, however, most clearly differentiate the borderline from the more neurotic individual. The relative ego strengths and underlying ego weaknesses are now examined briefly.

The Relative Ego Strengths

Reality testing. The strength here is that, on a surface level, and in day-to-day functioning, reality testing is basically intact. The weakness can emerge under stress and in very close interpersonal situations in which there is a tendency for this ego function to regress, sometimes leading to brief psychotic episodes. Regarding symptomatology, it is sometimes difficult to differentiate these regressions from other psychotic episodes. What does distinguish these episodes is their brevity (from minutes up to a day or two), their spontaneous reversibility, and their relationship to clear-cut precipitating events. These transient psychotic episodes under stress are allowable but certainly not mandatory to making the diagnosis of borderline.

Thought processes. The strength is that, in day-to-day functioning and in structured situations, thought processes are predominantly secondary processes. The weakness can come about under stress and in unstructured situations (such as projective psychological testing) when primary process sometimes emerges. Although there is the tendency to find a psychological test pattern of secondary process on the Wechsler Adult Intelligence Scale (WAIS) and primary process on the Rorschach, there is much disagreement as to how frequently this test pattern will actually be found in the borderline patient.

Interpersonal relations. The strength here is that the borderline patient often seems to do adequately in terms of interpersonal relations. On the surface, he or she seems to "relate" to others, can have many acquaintances, and sometimes can maintain long-term relationships. Weaknesses emerge when, under closer scrutiny, it becomes apparent that the relationships are often characterized by a lack of depth and a lack of concern for the other individual as a person. The other person is seen as someone who can be used to meet the borderline patient's needs rather than as a person in his or her own right. Empathy is lacking, and the borderline individual often vacillates between superficial relationships and intense, dependent relationships that are marred by primitive defenses. In their relationships, borderline patients are often very sensitive to real or imagined abandonments and to real or perceived slights, rejections, rebuffs, disappointments, and failures.

Adaptation to reality. The strength here is that adaptation is often superficially intact. The borderline patient may seem of normal appearance and may seem to display adequate achievement in work or school. Weaknesses in this area emerge when, under closer scrutiny, it is noted that the adaptation is far from optimal. There are certain "exceptional" borderlines who can maximize certain strengths and adapt adequately over time, particularly in structured settings. These individuals often do quite well professionally while displaying much more chaos in their social lives. Typically, these people display certain marked ego strengths together with their weaknesses. Strengths often include high intelligence and the ability to use obsessive-compulsive defenses. This exceptional group, more than others, seeks out intensive psychotherapy.

The Underlying Ego Weaknesses

Poor impulse control and poor frustration tolerance. Invariably, the borderline patient displays the combination of poor frustration tolerance and poor impulse control. There is an inability to delay, a demand for immediate gratification, and a proclivity to act out under stress. To make matters more difficult, these characteristics are sometimes combined with a sense of entitlement. These difficulties frequently present themselves clinically by a tendency for states of disruptive anger, by use of drugs and alcohol to avoid frustration and obtain temporary gratification, and by an inclination to flee the work or interpersonal situation under stress. There is a tendency in some for impulsive suicidal threats and attempts, in addition to other self-destructive behavior.

The proclivity to use primitive ego defenses. In day-to-day functioning, the borderline patient, with marked individual variation, uses a combination of mature, neurotic, immature, and borderline defenses. Under stress, he or she displays a marked tendency to rely on borderline defenses. In marked regressions, he or she may also use psychotic defenses. Borderline defenses include splitting, primitive idealization, projection, projective identification, primitive denial, omnipotence, and devaluation. Primitive defenses are thought to include, in addition to these borderline defenses, acting out and the psychotic defenses.

Splitting refers to the tendency to view individuals and things (external objects) as either all good or all bad. Primitive idealization, devaluation, and omnipotence are viewed as derivatives of splitting. Primitive idealization is the positive component of the split directed toward an external object (or individual). The external object is viewed as all good not for any realistic reason but because the patient has the need or wish to see it as all good. Devaluation is the negative component of the split, directed toward an external object or toward the self. Omnipotence is the positive component of the split directed toward the self. Although many patients make rapid reversals from one side of the split to the other, particularly under stress, others tend to maintain their primitive idealizations and devaluations over long periods of time.

The denial characteristic of most borderline patients is of a primitive, global, and blatantly unrealistic nature, somewhat akin to splitting. Two events or facts are clearly remembered in consciousness, yet one is totally denied or ignored. Alternatively, an event or fact is clearly remembered, but there is total disregard of its implications, consequences, and relevance.

Projective identification is the most confusing of all borderline defenses. One does not need to use the term *projective identification*; one can use other language to describe the same phenomenon. However, this term has become commonplace, and it behooves one to understand it. The most common usage of projective identification is as follows (Goldstein, 1991). A projection is followed by an interpersonal interaction in which the projector actively pressures the recipient to think, feel, and act in accordance with the projection. It is this coercive interpersonal interaction that is the essential feature of projective identification. What is confusing about the term is the varying definitions of projection, whether the process must include a blurring of self and object representations, and whether a reinternalization process (occurring after the interpersonal interaction) should be part of the concept.

Identity diffusion. This term refers to an identity that is not integrated or cohesive but diffuse. It is an identity based on multiple contradictory, unintegrated self-images. Correspondingly, there are multiple contradictory unintegrated object images. At one time, one self-image is evoked, and, at another time, a different one is invoked. The same applies to object images. Neither a comprehensive view of the self nor such a view of objects has ever been attained. As a result, borderline individuals are unable to describe themselves or others in a meaningful way. There is a lack of temporal continuity regarding the self and others, along with an overall distortion of the perceptions of self and others. Sometimes the borderline patient experiences an inner lack or void, a sense of emptiness or depletion. Various types of stimulating activities, including self-mutilating behaviors, are sometimes used to rid oneself of these painful feelings. Other terms frequently used to describe this problem include *lack of an integrated self-concept*, *lack of a sense of self*, *lack of a real self*, *lack of a stable identity*, and *lack of a coherent sense of self.*

Affective instability. The presence of irritability; intense affect, usually depressive or hostile; anger as the main affect experienced; and depressed, lonely, and empty feelings are frequently emphasized. Aggression is not used in constructive, ego-syntonic, adaptive ways, such as sublimations, work, recreation, and enjoyment. Thus, the aggression often breaks through directly in disruptive ways, such as outbursts of anger and rage, or the aggression is defended against in maladaptive ways and results in other ego-dystonic affect states such as depression, boredom, and emptiness. Often there can be rapid and dramatic swings from one affect state to another.

The borderline diagnosis. One does not expect patients in the borderline grouping to demonstrate all four ego strengths and all four ego weaknesses. In contrast, one looks at the overall pattern of ego strengths and weaknesses and establishes into which large grouping (normal-neurotic, narcissistic, borderline, or psychotic) the patient best fits.

5. What Are the Characteristics of the Narcissistic Grouping?

The main focus here is on the differentiation of the narcissistic grouping from the borderline. Differentiation of these two groupings, along with the issue of whether narcissistic individuals represent a subgroup of the borderline grouping, remains controversial. The two predominant experts on narcissistic patients, Kernberg and Kohut, are not in agreement here. Kohut (1971, 1977) classifies the borderline patient with the psychotic and clearly differentiates these individuals from the narcissistic. Kernberg (1975, 1980, 1984), in contrast, divides narcissistic patients into three groups, one of which clearly falls into the borderline grouping and two of which do not. Although it is true that a number of individuals classified as narcissistic do fall into the borderline grouping, there appears to be a group of narcissistic patients with ego profiles somewhat similar to the borderline, yet subtly but distinctly different under close scrutiny. This group of individuals includes both Kohut's narcissistic patients and Kernberg's "healthier" narcissistic individuals. It is this group that fits into the narcissistic grouping described here. The narcissistic grouping falls between the neurotic and borderline in degree of psychopathology.

The main differences between patients in the narcissistic grouping and those in the borderline grouping are in the areas of identity diffusion, impulse control/frustration tolerance, and affective instability. Regarding identity, instead of an unintegrated and unstable identity (identity diffusion), the narcissistic patient has an integrated but pathological identity based on a grandiose self. This identity, although clearly pathological, is basically stable and cohesive and resists disruptive fragmentation.

Regarding impulse control/frustration tolerance and stability of affects, these ego functions are relatively stronger in the narcissistic patient than in the borderline, yet still sensitive to regression. This sensitivity is not global, as with borderline individuals, but is limited to the area of narcissistic vulnerability. Narcissistic patients have highly labile self-esteems. They are exceedingly sensitive to perceived slights, rejections, rebuffs, disappointments, and failures. Reactions to these perceived threats are commonly seen both within and outside of the therapy hour. The slights, no matter how subtle, often produce very uncomfortable feelings, along with disruptive behavior. The patient may become bored or depressed, feel dull and empty, begin to do work without vigor or zest, lose initiative, begin to brood, or become preoccupied with his or her body. Sometimes he or she may experience embarrassment, shame, humiliation, or rage. It is especially in regard to those affects that compensatory defenses may ensue. These include various kinds of stimulating and dangerous acting-out behavior, perverse sexuality, and drug and alcohol abuse. To this pronounced sensitivity to slights and rejections, with the corresponding onset of uncomfortable feelings and disruptive behavior, is assigned the name *narcissistic vulnerability*.

Regarding the other ego functions, there are fewer differences between narcissistic and borderline patients. Interpersonal relations, intact superficially, are sometimes maintained to a somewhat better degree in the narcissistic patient, yet are nonetheless distorted by narcissistic configurations. As in the borderline grouping, relationships are characterized as need fulfilling; there is a striking lack of depth and empathy and a lack of concern for the other individual as a person. The narcissistic patient views people in accordance with his or her own needs, easily rejecting and disregarding others without feeling when frustrated.

Adaptation to reality is often better than in the borderline grouping, in relation to narcissistic patients' stable but pathological identity (vs. identity diffusion), but is usually lacking in comparison with the normal-neurotic. Reality testing and thought processes are generally well maintained, with little propensity to regression. Defenses are similar to those of the borderline patient. Primitive idealization, omnipotence, devaluation, and splitting are especially used, both in day-to-day functioning and under stress. Regressions to psychotic defenses are not characteristic.

Narcissistic patients do not uniformly display all of the ego weaknesses detailed. Some of these patients are best noted for their feelings of grandiosity, whereas others are mainly characterized by their problems with narcissistic vulnerability. Sometimes the narcissistic traits are not overt and are initially difficult to diagnose. There are many "closet narcissists" whose problems become apparent only in select circumstances, often within the context of long-term relationships. In fact, the narcissistic diagnosis, at times, can be difficult to make in a routine diagnostic assessment. This difficulty in initial diagnosis is in marked contrast to the other three large groupings, in which the diagnosis is more readily apparent.

6. What Are the Characteristics of the Psychotic Grouping?

In direct contrast to the normal-neurotic grouping, the hallmark of the psychotic grouping is that of poor ego functioning. Despite this generalization, many psychotic individuals show good ego functioning in a number of areas.

The basic deficit of the psychotic patient is a weakness in reality testing. In fact, psychosis has often been defined as a defect in this ego function. Psychotic individuals, when unmedicated, are characterized either by a constant problem in reality testing or by a marked vulnerability to regress in this ego function under stress. The latter problem can be demonstrated by a continual vacillation in displaying and concealing problems in reality testing. There are some psychotic individuals who typically are able to conceal their problems in this area, continually expending energy to prevent distortions in reality testing from surfacing. These latter psychotic individuals present a healthier appearance, only occasionally displaying defects in reality testing. These patients are sometimes difficult to differentiate from borderline individuals who regress in reality testing under obvious stress.

A second basic problem in the ego functioning of the psychotic individual involves thought processes. A consistent use of primary process thinking or a marked vulnerability to easily regress in this area is indicative of a psychotic process. It should be noted, however, that a number of psychotic patients do not show this pattern.

With marked variation, the psychotic individual typically shows problems in a number of other ego functions. Interpersonal relations are sometimes characterized by a lack of interest, withdrawal, and apathy. At other times, problems are more in accordance with those of the borderline grouping. Difficulties in adaptation to reality vary in accordance with the extent of the psychotic process. Often there are obvious problems in impulse control and frustration tolerance and with affective instability. The usual defensive pattern of the psychotic individual includes a combination of all defenses (mature, neurotic, immature, borderline, and psychotic) in day-to-day functioning, with a proclivity to the use of psychotic defenses under stress. The syndrome of identity diffusion is typical, as is the tendency to fuse self-representations and object representations.

7. Is Placing Patients into These Large Groupings Useful for Therapy?

Placing patients into one of the four large groupings is invaluable regarding psychotherapy, because the grouping dictates the type of therapy. Although there is overlap, different therapeutic strategies, approaches, and techniques are used for the different groupings. These strategies, approaches, and techniques are detailed and elaborated throughout this book.

The Therapists

8. Who Are the Psychotherapists?

Psychotherapists typically include psychiatrists, psychologists, clinical social workers, nurses, counselors of various sorts, and members of the clergy. As if this group did not offer the prospective patient enough choice, other less trained individuals do psychotherapy as well.

It is sometimes difficult to know what attracts so many people to the field. At a time when insurance reimbursement is declining, the mental health profession is becoming more saturated and more competitive. It is amazing how many high-powered professionals, including people with various kinds of PhDs, enroll in social work school or analogous programs with the intent of becoming psychotherapists.

Although most psychotherapists are well-intentioned, dedicated, and stable individuals, a number do not meet these criteria. Some people enter the field in attempts, often unconscious, to solve their own internal conflicts. Although these conflicts are often basically neurotic, they can also be at the narcissistic or even borderline level. Some of these latter individuals, if they are able to understand and control their most difficult problem areas, actually can make good therapists, especially for borderline patients. These therapists often easily empathize and resonate with such patients in ways that others cannot. Yet, they are subject to overidentification, to being too maternal and giving, and to boundary violations and other forms of acting out. The importance of their own intensive psychotherapy looms large for these therapists.

9. What Are Some of the Problems Inherent in Doing Psychotherapy?

Psychotherapy, when done well, although fascinating and intellectually stimulating, can also be quite tedious, grueling, and demanding. One of the most difficult aspects of this work is the constant challenge of facing one's own problems and differentiating them from those of the patients. Projecting one's problems onto patients, taking out one's anger on them, treating them in ways that one always wished to be treated oneself, and using them for one's own gratification are unfortunately common, although often very subtle, tendencies in some therapists. More overt problems such as boundary violations and sexual acting out are less common but more publicized. To avoid these occupational hazards, the therapist needs to take every opportunity to understand himself or herself as thoroughly as possible.

Isolation is another typical difficulty, one that often accompanies long hours of work. Professional activities outside of therapy hours, regular contact and discussions with colleagues, and various types of recreational activities help counteract this problem.

10. How Important Is One's Personal Therapy or Psychoanalysis?

One's own psychoanalysis or intensive psychotherapy is crucial in allowing one to understand one's own problems and to minimize their influence in the psychotherapy process. The most intense psychotherapy that one can reasonably undertake (usually psychoanalysis) should be a requirement for all therapists. For whatever reason, in the present climate, psychoanalysis is not as frequently recommended as in the past. In some settings in which students had been previously told that one's own analysis was indispensable for becoming a therapist, they are now told that analysis or intensive psychotherapy is recommended. This leads to the question of whether analytically oriented psychotherapy can substitute for psychoanalysis as a vehicle for self-understanding in therapists. Such therapy, when conducted by a highly skilled therapist, can be immensely rewarding and helpful. Still, I feel that therapists (in the normal-neurotic large grouping) shortchange themselves and their patients unless they select the therapy that provides the maximum potential for self-understanding.

There is no denying that there are therapists for whom psychoanalysis is not the treatment of choice. For psychotherapists with a number of borderline conflicts, analytically oriented psychotherapy is usually the preferred recommendation. Many therapists with narcissistic conflicts do well in psychoanalysis, although some do better with an analytically oriented approach.

11. What Kinds of Personal Characteristics and Experiences Help Make a Good Therapist?

A reasonable degree of stability is obviously necessary. Qualities such as concern, dedication, integrity, conscientiousness, competence, high intelligence, psychological-mindedness, and empathy are also of importance. It is useful for the therapist to have experienced a certain amount of suffering, depression, and neurotic conflict. Such suffering usually aids both understanding and empathy. A reflective, thoughtful individual, on the pessimistic to realistic side, is a plus. Too much optimism is associated with denial and does not bode well for understanding conflict. It is also important to be able to listen without the need to intervene and to be able to bear criticism and hostility without the need to retaliate. Intuition and creativity are additional assets for doing psychotherapy.

12. What About the Role of Life Experience?

Life experience is another important aspect of being an effective psychotherapist. With that in mind, a middle-aged woman with teenage children would have an advantage over someone in her early 20s just out of social work school. Life experience increases the number of circumstances with which one has familiarity, enhances one's ability to empathize, and provides one with a broader perspective.

There used to be the argument among psychiatrists that the medical school experience enhanced one's ability to be a therapist, because doctors acquired skill in handling life and death situations. This is a variant of the life experience factor applied to emergency situations. There is some truth, I think, to the idea that psychiatrists are often more comfortable with emergency situations in terms of both knowing when to act and doing so. Whether that experience results in one being a better psychotherapist is doubtful.

13. What Is the Role of Training and Supervision?

Given reasonable stability, favorable personal characteristics, an understanding of oneself via a personal analysis, and life experience, one needs to learn theory and technique via courses and reading and to obtain practical experience with excellent supervision. In the past, psychiatric residency and psychology PhD programs provided this type of training, but the trend has been for many of those programs to deemphasize the psychotherapy component. Two- to three-year formal programs in psychotherapy, often offered by psychoanalytic institutions, now help fill this void. It is theoretically possible for one to learn on one's own, but only the exceptional therapist can do this well. There is a tendency to learn what one likes and to avoid what one dislikes; as a result, self-learned therapists often have gaps in their knowledge.

Continual reading of relevant material is important for both beginning and experienced therapists. Although reading and didactic learning can never replace practical experience, they represent a necessary adjunct. To do therapy well, one must have a solid theoretical base. Technique needs to be learned via courses, reading, and supervision. The more of all three, the better.

14. How Long Does It Take to Become an Effective Therapist?

It takes years of experience for one to develop into a reasonably effective therapist. How many years is an open question; I have often heard 10 mentioned. Obviously, it depends on the therapist and the amount of experience per year. Again, life experience and personal characteristics play a role. Actually, psychotherapy is a process of continual, never-ending learning. Every additional experience adds to one's abilities.

15. Is It Useful to See a Variety of Patients, or Is It Better to Specialize?

Early in one's career, it is advisable to take on a variety of different types of patients. Rather than turn down patients with problems with which one is uncomfortable, it is useful to experience treatment with these individuals. Many therapists are surprised at the positive experiences they have with patients whom they would have naturally avoided. Later in one's career is a better time to begin to specialize, after one has sufficient time and experience in being a "generalist." My own experience is that many of the patients whom I had initial inclinations to avoid turned out to be very rewarding people with whom to work. These included patients I initially disliked, ones I thought would be too difficult, and ones with problems with which I had minimal experience.

16. Do Some Therapists Work Better with Specific Types of Patients?

Although I have emphasized the value of all therapists obtaining experience with a variety of patients, inevitably certain therapists are better able to work with certain groups of patients. With regard to the large groupings, those therapists who are best at listening without rapid intervention, who can tolerate being relatively passive, and who are most interested in technical skills do well with neurotic patients. Those therapists who are comfortable with being both idealized and devalued, who can easily recognize when that is happening, and who are tolerant with others' self-centeredness, sense of entitlement, and aloofness do well with narcissistic patients. Therapists with warmth, empathy, and flexibility, in addition to technical skills; who are comfortable with a more interactive approach; and who can withstand harsh attacks on themselves, even in areas in which they are especially sensitive, do well with borderline patients. Finally, therapists who have much patience, who are nonintrusive but able to intervene in emergency situations, who are not tempted to impose their own ideals and aspirations on the patient, and who can maintain a positive attitude, do well with psychotic patients.

The preceding are only generalizations. Most of the characteristics noted are quite useful when dealing with any patient, regardless of large grouping. Some therapists have many of the characteristics just listed, are able to alter their approaches with different individuals, and do well with a wide variety of patients. Others, although they might do exceptionally well with select groups of patients, do poorly with others. They will, it is hoped, come to realize this and act accordingly.

17. Is the Sex or Ethnic Background of the Therapist Important?

Often, a patient is interested in seeing a therapist of a specific sex or a specific ethnic group. Yet, with regard to the ultimate success of the therapy, sex and ethnic group play small roles in comparison with the experience, expertise, and personality of the therapist. This is not to say that there will not be differences in the unfolding of the transference and in the timing of the emergence of various issues. Regarding transference, patients ultimately form maternal and paternal transferences to therapists of either sex.

Feeling that women are more empathic and sensitive to their needs, a number of women request female therapists. This choice is often based on comfort rather than what might be best for the patient. In some cases, even though the patient is more comfortable with a woman therapist, working through her conflicts might be better accomplished with a man. If I am asked to make a referral in this type of circumstance, I always discuss the pros and cons of seeing a woman versus a man and offer my perspective; however, I always proceed with a referral in accordance with the patient's ultimate request. Regarding comfort with specific ethnic groups, analogous thinking applies.

There are a few instances in which gender is important. With certain adolescents, in therapies in which the process of identification is anticipated to be important, therapists of the same gender are sometimes preferable. In patients who have been brutalized and abused in childhood, a therapist of the opposite gender of that of the abuser might be advantageous. Sometimes when there has been an early death of a parent, a therapist of the same sex as the lost parent can be helpful.

The Psychotherapy

18. How Can Psychotherapy Be Classified?

The different types of psychotherapy can be conceptualized on a continuum, with the most insight-oriented and exploratory types at one end and the most supportive types at the other (Goldstein, 1985, 1996). Five types of psychotherapy along this continuum can be differentiated: psychoanalysis, analytically oriented psychotherapy, modified analytically oriented psychotherapy, dynamically oriented psychotherapy, and supportive psychotherapy.

19. What Is Psychoanalysis, and for Whom Is It Indicated?

The dynamically based psychotherapies are, in part, derivatives of psychoanalysis. Thus, although the focus in this book is not on psychoanalysis, an understanding of this process as background is useful. Psychoanalysis will first be examined in the traditional or classical way.

In traditional psychoanalysis, the patient comes for regularly scheduled sessions, four or five times a week, for a number of years. There is no contact between patient and psychoanalyst outside of the appointments. Sessions are typically conducted with the patient lying on the psychoanalytic couch and the analyst sitting comfortably behind the patient. Patients are instructed simply to free associate; that is, they are to do their best to say whatever comes to mind and not eliminate any thoughts for any reason. They are particularly cautioned to try not to eliminate thoughts because they think the thoughts are silly or irrelevant, because they are fearful that the analyst will disapprove, because they want to avoid uncomfortable feelings associated with the thoughts, or because the thoughts relate to the analyst. Often, this is all of the instruction the patient is given.

As patients attempt to free associate, various resistances within them make the process difficult. As these resistances are noticed by the analyst, he or she will comment on them in an effort to help the patient overcome them and continue to free associate. The analyst initially confines his or her comments to these resistances and to helping patients elaborate and expand on what he or she is saying. Throughout the psychoanalysis, the analyst's comments remain of a very specific nature. They are directed specifically to the analytic process and are usually in the nature of clarifications and interpretations. Almost all comments serve the singular purpose of enhancing the psychoanalytic process. Psychoanalysis works as a very gradual process during which aspects of oneself that were previously unconscious become conscious. The transference is used as the primary and most effective forum for this process. In order to provide a setting in which the patient can most easily transfer his feelings onto the analyst, the analyst has to be seen in a neutral way. It is for this reason that the analyst confines his or her remarks to clarifications and interpretations regarding the psychoanalytic process as exclusively as possible. The analyst is thus able to maintain a "neutral" position while still being warm, empathic, and concerned about the patient.

Aided by the frequency and the intensity of the sessions, by the use of the couch and the basic process of free association, and by the maintenance of a neutral position by the analyst, a progressively intense transference becomes established. This intense transference involves patients displacing or "transferring" onto the analyst feelings and thoughts that were originally directed toward the important people of their early childhood. The transference includes not only these feelings and thoughts but also defenses against them. It is based on both the actual and fantasized past, as experienced by the patient. The patient's pathological and nonpathological personality traits, as well as his or her symptoms, all based on intrapsychic conflict, are activated in the psychoanalytic process and become an integral part of the transference. It is the establishment and working through of the transference that is crucial to the attainment of insight and that most clearly differentiates psychoanalysis from other forms of psychotherapy.

Continuing to confine himself or herself basically to clarifications and interpretations, the analyst begins to comment on aspects of the transference about which the patient is unaware, especially when these aspects appear as resistances to the analytic process. The analyst correlates what is happening in the transference with the patient's current interactions and relationships with significant others and, especially, with the patient's significant interactions and relationships in childhood. In this way, the analyst helps patients begin to learn about previously unconscious aspects of themselves, including those aspects that have afforded them the most difficulty. As patients expand their awareness in this way and gain insight, they are gradually able to make adaptive adjustments and changes in their psychopathology, personalities, and lives. The permanency of these changes can be attributed to underlying "structural change," that is, changes in the alignment and relationship of the id, ego, and superego. The analytic process is not smooth; rather, it is characterized by continual resistances and continual progressions and regressions, but with a gradual overall advancement.

Gill (1954), in his classic article, defined psychoanalysis as a therapeutic technique, employed by a neutral analyst, that permits and results in the development of an intense regressive transference, with the ultimate resolution of this transference by the technique of interpretation alone. There are basically three aspects of this definition that distinguish analysis from other forms of psychotherapy: the analyst's neutrality, the development and resolution of the transference, and the emphasis on interpretation as the primary therapeutic intervention. It is these three aspects that many (Kernberg, 1980; Ticho, 1970) focus on when differentiating psychoanalysis from other forms of psychotherapy. Given this definition, for analysis to be successful, the patient's personality traits, symptoms, and psychopathology must become activated in the treatment situation; enter into a specific transference with the analyst; and be worked through and resolved in the analytic process by interpretation alone. Thus, a critical criterion for analyzability is that such a transference can be formed and resolved without disruptive fragmentation or regression. The basically neurotic individual meets this criterion; the basically psychotic individual does not. Kohut (1971, 1984) believes that the narcissistic personality meets this criterion, although some disagree. Whether the borderline individual meets this criterion depends largely on one's criteria for the diagnosis of the borderline patient.

The preceding description of psychoanalysis, traditional and classical as it is, remains a good one for comparing psychoanalysis to other forms of psychotherapy. In contemporary times, however, many take exception to aspects of the traditional view. The positivist position of the classical school, where the analyst is thought capable of standing outside the interaction with the patient in a search for objective truth, has been challenged by newer perspectives. These include relational models, self-psychology, intersubjectivity, social constructivism, and postmodern thinking. Many analysts of the classical school have changed some of their views in accordance with these newer perspectives.

Thus there is a shift from viewing analysis as a process in which the patient transfers his feelings onto a "blank screen," to a process that is more interactional, interpersonal, and subjective in nature, where there is a mingling of transference and countertransference between patient and analyst. The analyst, as well as the patient, is viewed as a unique individual, with his own theory of how analysis works, his own idiosyncrasies, and his own past, all of which contribute to the unfolding of the psychoanalytic process. Some posit the analyst, in addition to the patient, as involved in the construction of the transference. Many integrate the positivist with more contemporary approaches by conceptualizing the patient as coming to analysis with preexisting feelings, ideas, and personality traits, which he transfers onto the analyst, who also has preexisting feelings, ideas, and personality traits that influence and skew the psychoanalytic process.

With these changing perspectives, the concepts of the authority of the analyst and that of neutrality have been questioned. Analysis is sometimes viewed more as a process between equals than between an uninformed patient and a knowledgeable authority. Some (Hoffman, 1996) emphasize a dialectic between the analyst as an authority and the analyst as a person like the patient. Neutrality is now uniformly viewed as an impossible state to attain. Yet, despite this, many regard it as a desirable ideal to which they should try to approximate. Others (Renik, 1996) view it as an antiquated and even harmful concept, advocating the acceptance of the "nonneutral," subjective analyst.

The basic task of analysis, the attainment of insight, or the discovery of that which was previously unconscious, via a reliving in the transference, has also been challenged. The emphasis on empathic attunement and immersion, advocated by some as a means to attain insight, has been posited by others as an end in itself. Some (Renik, 1996; Hoffman, 1996) believe that learning in analysis takes place dialectically. Dialectics between the authority of the analyst and the analyst as a person similar to the patient, between the analyst's role-defined behavior and his spontaneous expressive participation, between a positivist and intersubjective approach, and between modern and postmodern thinking have been noted as important aspects of the psychoanalytic process. Some feel that patients learn dialectically by contrasting their thinking with new alternate perspectives proposed by the analyst. A postmodern influence focuses on factors such as uncertainty, ambiguity, ambivalence, fragmentation, irony, cynicism, and relativism.

These contemporary ideas might well be confusing to the beginner; they can also be confusing to some sophisticated and experienced therapists. They are included here, so that one can understand the complexity and challenges of the field today.

Psychoanalysis is basically designed for individuals in the normal-neurotic grouping. These individuals include those with symptomatic neuroses but more frequently are those primarily with character (or personality) pathology. They usually suffer from chronic problems that, although far from disabling, interfere with their attaining their life goals, maximizing their potentials, and leading basically content lives. These individuals suffer from a wide assortment of character problems, including those of obsessive-compulsive, hysterical, depressive, masochistic, narcissistic, and mixed natures.

Although the character pathology varies markedly, these individuals commonly present themselves in one of several ways. One of the most common initial presentations is that of the individual who, although doing well on the job and having many friends, is unable to form sustaining, long-term, intimate personal relationships. Marriage is a goal, but something is stopping the individual from attaining this goal. Such people realize that their problems are chronic and deep seated and lie within themselves. Often they are somewhat sophisticated about psychoanalysis and specifically come with that treatment modality in mind. They frequently, although not always, suffer from sexual difficulties, along with varying degrees of anxiety and depression, in addition to their presenting complaints.

A second common initial presentation is that of patients who, although performing acceptably at work, feel that something is holding them back and stopping them from living up to their potentials. There may be overt problems with their peers or boss, and there may be anxiety about succeeding. They also have come to realize that their problems are chronic, deep seated, and within themselves. They may or may not, in addition, have problems in maintaining long-term, intimate relationships and may or may not suffer accompanying anxiety or depression.

For individuals who have psychopathology mainly at the neurotic level and who suffer from deep-seated character problems, most obviously manifested in failures in maintaining long-term intimate relationships or in failures in maximizing their potential at work, psychoanalysis is the treatment of choice. This is also the case for individuals with chronic symptomatic neuroses. For individuals who present clearcut narcisstic problems, psychoanalysis, although recommended by some, remains controversial. Among individuals in the borderline grouping, psychoanalysis is generally considered only for a selected minority. Psychoanalysis is generally not considered for individuals in the psychotic grouping.

20. What Is Analytically Oriented Psychotherapy and for Whom Is It Indicated?

This book uses the terms *analytically oriented psychotherapy* and *dynamically oriented psychotherapy* to describe two distinctly different, yet related, types of therapy. Differentiation of these two types of therapy, although not routinely advocated, has obvious advantages. This will become apparent as one reads this book.

Analytically oriented psychotherapy involves regularly scheduled sessions, usually two but sometimes three a week, held for varying periods of time. As in psychoanalysis, there is basically no contact between patient and psychotherapist outside of the appointments. Sessions are typically conducted with the patient and therapist sitting across from each other in comfortable chairs. Patients are usually told that the sessions are theirs, that they can talk about whatever they choose. In addition to discussing topics of their choice, patients are encouraged to report seemingly extraneous thoughts and fantasies that occur to them during the sessions. As in psychoanalysis, areas of typical resistance to such discussion are often mentioned. Thus, the trappings of analytically oriented psychotherapy are both similar to and different from those of psychoanalysis.

Although the trappings are somewhat different, the therapist attempts to conduct analytically oriented psychotherapy in a manner as similar as possible to that used in psychoanalysis. He or she tries to remain neutral (in the modern sense of the word, as described in Question 27), relies on clarifications and interpretations as much as possible, and tries to make maximum therapeutic use of the transference. Just as in psychoanalysis, the therapist comments on resistances, tries to correlate the transference with current interactions and significant childhood relationships, and attempts to help patients to understand gradually those aspects of themselves about which they are unaware. This is analytically oriented psychotherapy in its pure form.

Even this pure form of analytically oriented psychotherapy is often limited in effectiveness relative to psychoanalysis. The patient, constantly looking at the therapist and noting her or his expressions and mannerisms, "learns" more about the therapist than would be the case in psychoanalysis, and can have more difficulty "transferring" her or his feelings onto the therapist. Without the use of the couch, without the process of free association, and with less frequent sessions, the transference does not usually form with the same primitivity, intensity, or speed. The ability to form an intense transference varies markedly from patient to patient. Even at its "best," however, with patients in the normal-neurotic grouping, the quality of transference in analytically oriented psychotherapy is rarely on a par with that in psychoanalysis. Although analytically oriented psychotherapy can be quite effective, the lack of a fully developed intense transference can limit this form of psychotherapy.

Many individuals undergoing analytically oriented psychotherapy are very similar to those undergoing psychoanalysis. Time and financial limitations, fear of psychoanalysis per se, and lack of knowledge about the psychoanalytic process are the usual reasons that psychoanalysis proper is not chosen.

21. What is Modified Analytically Oriented Psychotherapy, and for Whom Is It Indicated?

Modified analytically oriented psychotherapy involves the same trappings as analytically oriented psychotherapy. Modifications are in the areas that differentiate psychoanalysis from the other forms of psychotherapy: the analyst's neutrality, the development and resolution of the transference, and the emphasis on interpretation as the primary therapeutic intervention. Modifications are initiated because of the psychopathology of the patient, which makes unmodified analytically oriented psychotherapy difficult or even impossible. Modified analytically oriented psychotherapy is ideally suited for many borderline individuals.

The area of least modification for borderline patients is the transference, which continues to be emphasized as the crucial forum through which the conflicts of the patient are resolved. This emphasis is especially suitable for these patients, because borderline individuals often form rapid and intense transferences even without the use of the couch. It is the rapid mobilization of the transference that distinguishes the typical borderline patient from the typical neurotic. The latter becomes involved with the transference at a slower and more gradual pace, sometimes with difficulty. The neutrality of the analyst is maintained, not so much regarding equidistance from id, ego, superego, and external reality but in the sense of the therapist being nonjudgmental, noncritical, and totally focused on the patient. Modifications regarding interventions vary greatly. In some borderline patients, there can be a preponderance of insight-orient interventions; in others, the focus switches to supportive techniques.

With the ability of many borderline patients to become rapidly involved with the therapist and the transference, the opportunity to use analytically oriented psychotherapy is clear. However, because of the borderline individual's ego weaknesses and propensity for overregression, the modified approach is usually necessary.

22. What Is Dynamically Oriented Psychotherapy, and for Whom Is It Indicated?

Dynamically oriented psychotherapy involves regularly scheduled sessions, often one but sometimes two a week, held for varying periods of time. There is little contact between patient and psychotherapist outside of the appointments. Sessions are always conducted with the patient and therapist sitting across from each other. Basically the same instructions are given to the patient as in analytically oriented psychotherapy, although sometimes the instruction to report seemingly extraneous material is omitted.

The main difference between dynamically oriented psychotherapy and analytically oriented psychotherapy is the downplaying of transference as a therapeutic modality in the former. Although transference reactions are noted, especially when they occur as resistances, the elaboration of the transference is not considered a major ingredient in this form of psychotherapy. Rather, the therapist and the patient focus much more exclusively on present-day interactions and relationships and their correlation to the patient's past. Patient and therapist together try to understand the patient's present-day interactions on the basis of her or his sensitivities, vulnerabilities, and distortions, which originate in the past. A positive therapeutic alliance is fostered, and the therapist is sometimes mildly idealized. Occasional suggestion and education are employed, along with clarifications and partial interpretations.

Dynamically oriented psychotherapy is found particularly useful by some psychotherapists for a selected group of patients, often psychotic but sometimes borderline, who present problems with the elaboration and working through of the transference. One group of borderline patients starts psychotherapy with a modified analytically oriented approach and then, after a reasonable therapeutic alliance has been established, switches to a dynamically oriented modality. Other psychotherapists routinely use dynamically oriented psychotherapy as their primary form of psychotherapy, both for patients who would benefit from a more analytically oriented approach and for those who would not.

Although dynamically oriented psychotherapy is found on the supportive end of the continuum, the degree of support varies in accordance with the therapist's choice of interventions. Thus, dynamically oriented psychotherapy can be used for neurotic individuals via mainly insight-oriented interventions. In contrast, it can be used for psychotic individuals through a preponderance of supportive interventions.

There is debate about what type of psychotherapy is best for neurotic patients who are not in psychoanalysis. One group favors simulating analysis as much as possible. A second group, noting the difficulty in attaining intense transference with neurotic patients in psychotherapy, favors using a dynamically oriented approach. Other therapists lean toward an analytically oriented modality for those neurotic patients, (often hysterical in personality type) who can form an intense transference in psychotherapy, while employing a more dynamically oriented model for those neurotic patients (often obsessive in personality type) who have greater difficulty here.

23. What Is Supportive Psychotherapy, and for Whom Is It Indicated?

In supportive psychotherapy, the patient comes for regularly scheduled sessions, usually once a week but sometimes more frequently, for varying but often lengthy periods. The principle underlying the number of sessions scheduled is virtually the opposite of that used in the more analytically oriented psychotherapies. In the latter approaches, increased sessions are used to promote intensity and regression. In supportive psychotherapy, the goal is to stop regression rather than to promote it. More frequent sessions are employed to stem untoward regression at times when the patient is having acute difficulty with some of his or her basic ego functions. When the patient is doing "well," a lower frequency of sessions, usually once a week, generally suffices. In supportive psychotherapy, contact between patient and therapist outside the sessions is promoted only to the extent that it is necessary to stem regression. Sessions are always conducted with the patient and therapist sitting across from each other. Patients are instructed simply to discuss those events in their life with which they are having difficulty.

Supportive psychotherapy is best suited for individuals with active disturbances in a number of their ego functions. This form of psychotherapy is indicated for a large group of basically psychotic individuals, although another group of psychotic patients can benefit more from dynamically oriented psychotherapy, at least some of the time. Supportive psychotherapy is also used by some in the treatment of selected borderline individuals. This form of psychotherapy is sometimes supplemented by psychiatric medication.

The purpose of supportive psychotherapy is to help build up the patient's weak ego functions (hence the often-used term *ego building*). For this purpose, many types of therapeutic interventions are employed, including education, suggestion, clarification, reassurance, advice, and instruction, but not usually interpretation. For these interventions to be most successful, the maintenance of a positive transference and a therapeutic alliance is exceptionally important. For this reason, the transference is usually not discussed unless it represents a resistance. Likewise, transference distortions are often rapidly corrected by education and reality testing. If this kind of psychotherapy is to proceed optimally, free association is not desirable. What is desirable is a detailed description of the day-to-day events that led to the patient's current difficulty with his or her ego functions. Hence, contrary to the more analytically oriented approaches, the focus is on the here and now, and reporting of weekly events is encouraged.

The initial goal of supportive psychotherapy is to help patients strengthen and maintain their ego functioning so that they can adapt adequately in day-to-day interactions. When patients begin to function acceptably in this realm, further goals are added. A second and more difficult goal is to help patients identify and accept those areas in which they are sensitive and vulnerable to regression. Once these areas are identified and accepted by the patient, he or she can begin to learn to deal with them more effectively and gradually respond to them by means other than regression.

The tasks of helping the patient to identify these stressful areas and then to deal more effectively with them can be very time consuming. As this work is pursued, the psychotherapeutic approach often becomes more exploratory and switches to a dynamically oriented framework. If and when the patient is able to make this switch, it is considered a welcome psychotherapeutic advance.

24. What Is Cognitive Therapy and for Whom Is It Indicated?

Cognitive therapy, traditionally used for the treatment of depression and anxiety, has become increasingly used for other problems as well. The framework for this type of treatment involves a combination of education and psychotherapy and includes the use of homework assignments. Cognitive therapy can be short or long term. Short-term therapy is generally used for patients suffering from discrete symptoms, including depression, hypomania, anxiety, phobias, paranoid states, hysteria, obsessions, and compulsions; long-term work is used for patients with characterological difficulties, including those in the borderline grouping.

Cognitive therapy works on a conscious level and thus demands a reasonable therapeutic alliance, sometimes termed the *collaborative relationship*. Transference plays little or no role, and the therapist is active, goal directed, and structured throughout, always operating in the present. A basic premise is that one's feelings and behavior are influenced in the here and now by one's thoughts. Thus, if one can change one's thoughts, one can correspondingly change one's feelings and behavior. Cognitive therapy attempts, in a systematized way, to help the patient accomplish this change.

There are various forms of cognitive therapy; the one described here is that of Schuyler (1991), based on the model of Beck (1976). I focus primarily on the short-term application. The initial sessions are used for history taking and rapid assessment, culminating in a time-limited contract. The focus then turns to helping the patient to learn the cognitive model. Therapy is conducted in a way that provides structure and aids the patient to gain mastery of that model.

Cognitive therapy focuses on automatic thoughts and schemas. Automatic thoughts are ones that occur in a stimulus-response manner. They are specific and concrete, invariably seen as plausible, and idiosyncratic to the individual. They can be viewed as first associations to any stimuli. Schemas are relatively enduring units of belief by which an individual governs his or her thinking and life. Automatic thoughts are derived from schemas and are more easily identified in a short period of time. Thus, short-term cognitive therapy focuses more on automatic thoughts, while longer term work focuses more on schemas.

Several examples of automatic thoughts follow. To the stimulus of a phone call from work: I must have done something wrong. To the stimulus of one's husband being late: He must have had an accident. To the stimulus of being greeted without a smile: He must not like me. Examples of schemas include the following: In order to be successful, my job must work out absolutely perfectly. In order to feel good about myself, I have to receive continual positive feedback.

Involving both the sessions and homework assignments, in which various kinds of record keeping are encouraged, cognitive therapy focuses on the identification of automatic thoughts. Once these automatic thoughts are identified, one looks for errors in related thinking. These errors can be classified into three major errors and four more specific distortions. The major errors are polarization, personalization, and overgeneralization; the specific distortions are selective abstraction, discounting, arbitrary inference, and catastrophizing. Polarization refers to viewing things as all good or all bad. Personalization involves viewing everything in terms of oneself. Overgeneralization means drawing conclusions well beyond the circumstances. Selective abstraction involves focusing on one detail out of context. Discounting refers to the inability to accept praise. An arbitrary inference means jumping to a conclusion. Catastrophizing refers to thinking in the worst possible terms.

One approach used both within and outside of therapy involves the three- to five-column technique. Lists are made, with the first column representing the situation (or stimulus), the second column representing the feeling, and the third representing the automatic thought. Later a fourth column, errors in thinking, is added. Still later, a fifth column, alternatives, helps the patient learn new ways of dealing with the situation.

Once the automatic thoughts are identified and related to the cognitive errors, the focus of the therapy transfers to "breaking the set," or stopping the automatic thinking. To help break the set, the therapist is quite active, offering analogies, providing disclosures from his or her own life, and using humor. Sometimes experiments are set up to test the validity of various assumptions related to the automatic thoughts.

The final stage of the therapy, that of generating alternatives (related to the fifth column), follows. Sometimes the suggestion is made that the old way of thinking has outlived its usefulness, and alternatives are needed. Alternatives can be understood with regard to the cognitive errors used. Thus, if the error is personalization, the alternative involves decentering. If the error is polarization, the alternative involves thinking in terms of "gray areas." If the error is overgeneralization, the alternative involves thinking in a way that demands specifying the data that account for the conclusions. A balance sheet is sometimes made in which the patient is encouraged to see the pros and cons of various alternatives. Sometimes reading is assigned.

Termination occurs at a set time, often with an evaluation and summary of the therapy. Sometimes a new contract is initiated for longer term work. Before termination, the patient is taught ways to carry out the therapeutic process independently. Follow-up appointments are typically made at increasingly longer intervals, starting at 1 month and then moving to 3- to 6-month periods.

CHAPTER

Larger Issues Regarding Psychotherapy

25. What Are the Larger Issues Regarding Psychotherapy?

The larger issues regarding psychotherapy refer to all types of therapy. They include the stability of the therapeutic environment, the neutrality and flexibility of the therapist, countertransference, empathy, the activity of the therapist, and the mechanism of change in psychotherapy.

26. What Is Meant by the Stability of the Therapeutic Environment?

Therapy needs to be carried out in a stable, consistent, and caring way in a safe, nonthreatening, and nonintrusive environment. The expectations of treatment should be clearly spelled out, discussed, and almost always followed. These include times of the sessions, missed appointments, payments, expectations regarding interactions between therapist and patient outside the sessions, and guidelines for the patient. Stability of the therapeutic environment implies that the therapist is competent, consistent, conscientious, concerned, empathic, and reasonable.

The stability of the therapeutic environment is important with all patients. The related concepts of good-enough mothering (Winnicott, 1958), the holding environment (Winnicott, 1965), and holding introjects (Adler, 1985) are mainly relevant with patients in the more troubled groupings. In these latter groupings, the stability of the therapeutic environment becomes instrumental in the gradual formation of a workable therapeutic alliance. In the normal-neurotic grouping, in contrast, a reasonable therapeutic alliance is a given.

27. Should the Therapist Be Neutral?

Technical neutrality classically refers to the therapist's position of equidistance from id, ego, superego, and external reality. The maintenance of neutrality is considered of most importance in those therapies in which the elaboration and resolution of the transference is primary. The neutral therapist strives to serve as a "blank screen," providing a setting most conducive for the displacement of feelings. This concept is most commonly used when working with patients in the normal-neurotic grouping. The concept of neutrality has become controversial. Contemporary thinkers view it as a theoretical ideal, impossible to attain in actuality. Some nevertheless favor attempting to approximate this unattainable ideal; others view the concept as antiquated and even harmful, advocating instead the acceptance of the "nonneutral," subjective therapist.

A useful modern concept of neutrality posits a neutral therapist as one who steers clear of judgment and criticism. He or she aims to use the therapy sessions to listen to and understand the patient and to make interventions based on this listening and understanding. This aim is emphasized and maintained throughout the treatment. Interventions always focus on the patient, his or her problems, and his or her life. Before intervening, the therapist thinks about how his or her intervention will influence the patient in the processes of internalization, ego building, and insight. The therapist will sometimes react emotionally to the patient; as much as possible, however, the therapist uses his or her reactions to understand the patient. Overidentification and excessive intrusion of the therapist's life into the therapy session are avoided. Neutrality here is compatible with a position of warmth, empathy, and concern.

28. Must the Therapist Be Flexible?

The flexibility of the therapist, often a minor factor in working with patients in the normal-neurotic grouping, becomes essential with more troubled patients. With these individuals, therapists must be flexible in terms of both approach and interventions. They have to be ready for the unpredictable, ready for new challenges, and able to be intuitive. Although they need to operate within a definite theoretical framework, they have to be able to make changes and adaptations within that framework.

Depending on the unfolding of the therapy, they might need to change from an insight-oriented approach to a more supportive approach, or vice versa. With some patients, therapists will have to oscillate in their methods over long periods of time; with others, they might have to permanently switch approaches. Always they need to be pragmatic and adaptive.

29. What Is Countertransference, and What Role Does It Play?

Countertransference has been defined in the narrow sense as the therapist's unconscious reactions to the patient's transference. In the broad sense, countertransference involves all emotional feelings by the therapist toward the patient, both conscious and unconscious. These feelings include reactions to the patient's transference, reactions to the patient's personality, and reactions actively elicited by the patient. Although some prefer the narrow definition when dealing with patients in the normal-neurotic grouping, there is somewhat of a consensus regarding the use of the broad definition when dealing with patients in the other three groupings.

With all patients, therapists must be on the alert for countertransference feelings. They need to keep countertransference acting out to a minimum and to use their countertransference to aid in their understanding and interventions. The therapist's own psychoanalysis is most relevant to his or her ability to deal with these feelings. No matter how well analyzed, however, all therapists will experience countertransference with all patients. Although often subtle with patients in the normal-neurotic grouping, countertransference can become more overt when the transference intensifies. It is the patients in the borderline and narcissistic groupings, however, who are most famous for creating difficult counter-transference situations.

Borderline patients are known for their ability to elicit emotional reactions in the therapist. It is not unusual for these patients to sense areas of weakness in the therapist and subtly attack the therapist in those areas. Sometimes the attacks are not so subtle. In projective identification, patients project their own feelings onto the therapist and then do everything in their power to "force" the therapist to accept the projections. Situations are created in which virtually every therapist responds. Thus, in working with patients in this grouping, the therapist is most vulnerable to acting out.

Gabbard and Wilkinson (1994) have categorized typical countertransference reactions to borderline patients. These reactions include guilt feelings, rescue fantasies, transgressions of professional boundaries, rage and hatred, helplessness, worthlessness, anxiety, and terror. Some of these feelings are inevitable when working with borderline patients; others occur more selectively in certain therapists working with certain borderline patients. Because of the danger of responding to one's countertransference with borderline patients, even the most experienced therapists need to be willing to partake in consultations with colleagues. Well-timed consultations can be invaluable, sometimes "saving" the therapy. With less experienced therapists, ongoing supervision is clearly useful.

Countertransference feelings with narcissistic patients occur in response to the patient's idealizations and devaluations. The latter, if sustained, can be excruciatingly painful and difficult to tolerate. Subtle devaluations, in the form of the patient acting as if the therapist does not exist, can lead to equally uncomfortable feelings. Sometimes these feelings are acted out in terms of early termination by the therapist. Idealizations are often more easily accepted. However, there is always the risk of their conversion to devaluations when the therapist does not live up to the patient's unreasonable expectations. Haughtiness, omnipotence, and grandiosity on the part of patients evoke strong negative feelings in a number of therapists.

Psychotic patients, particularly when they act passive and dependent or are unable to rapidly change, can elicit feelings of helplessness or dejection. A common countertransference acting out involves the therapist becoming too actively engaged in patients' lives, "forcing" his or her own values and attitudes on them and sometimes taking over ego functions that they are capable of managing themselves.

30. What Is the Role of Empathy?

An empathic stance, in which therapists identify with the patient to the extent that they attempt to experience what the patient feels, his or her way of thinking, and point of view, is of obvious value to the psychotherapeutic process. Not only does this stance help the therapist to understand the patient, it helps in establishing an environment in which trust is enhanced and the patient is free to talk about his or her innermost feelings and thoughts. Although important with all patients, an empathic stance has special value when dealing with patients in the narcissistic and borderline groupings.

Kohut (1971, 1977, 1984), of course, is responsible for the popularization of the concept of empathy. He believed in its use as an aid to understanding and insight, and not as a cure in itself. Focusing primarily on psychoanalysis, Kohut described the basic therapeutic unit as consisting of two steps: understanding and explaining. In the understanding phase, therapists verbalize to the patient that they grasp what he or she feels, demonstrating directly to the patient that he or she has been "understood." Then, in the explanatory phase, therapists use their theoretical knowledge to help the patient to become more objective about himself or herself and to gain dynamic and genetic insight. Whereas the understanding phase is basically a phase of empathic emersion, the explanatory phase is also based on empathy. The understanding phase helps patients accept themselves; the explanatory phase helps them become more objective about themselves while continuing to accept themselves. With certain vulnerable individuals, the understanding phase needs emphasis for much of the therapy; even here, however, the explanatory phase is eventually needed to effect permanent change.

31. How Active Should the Therapist Be?

Jokes are made about the passive analyst, attentively sitting and listening while the patient does the bulk of the talking. Yet, a position not dissimilar to this is sometimes reasonable when working with patients in the normal-neurotic grouping. This posture enhances both careful listening and the unfolding and development of the transference. Actually, this position is not as passive as it seems; the therapist, although relatively quiet, is very active in his or her attentive listening for the purpose of understanding.

When dealing with patients in the narcissistic grouping, a relatively passive posture is also frequently helpful, but for a different reason. This group of patients often views interventions as unwanted intrusions. Very sensitive to being dependent, controlled, or violated, these patients react negatively and angrily to many interventions. Especially in the early stage of therapy, these patients do better with a more silent approach, sometimes with minimal therapeutic activity. Later in the therapy, when the patient becomes comfortable and a reasonable therapeutic alliance has been formed, the therapist can become more active. The principle here is not to do what the patient wants but to promote a therapeutic alliance that will best facilitate the psychotherapy.

In contrast, a second group of narcissistic patients benefits from increased activity by the therapist. This group suffers from feelings such as emptiness, nothingness, and apathy related to childhoods lacking in excitement, vitality, and stimulation. A more silent therapist can revive and enhance those uncomfortable feelings, helping to create a therapeutic environment that resembles that of the early childhood. A more interactive approach can lead to a more comfortable milieu for the patient, again enhancing the chances of eventually achieving a reasonable therapeutic alliance.

When dealing with borderline patients, it is again helpful to take a more active approach, both talking more and using more facial expression. This is particularly useful with those patients lacking in trust and self-esteem and having negative self-concepts. These patients respond to relative silences or to ambiguous comments by feeling criticized, slighted, or rejected. They respond this way either during the therapy hour or as delayed reactions after the session. They often fantasize that the therapist thinks they are stupid, doesn't like them, prefers others, or doesn't want to see them anymore. Sometimes the fantasies are more ominous and paranoid. These fantasies can lead to very uncomfortable feeling states with acting out.

Thus, the therapist is best off initially with an interactive approach, with many clarifications, and as little ambiguity as possible. Later in the therapy, as the therapeutic alliance becomes consolidated, a gradual decrease in activity is often warranted. An interactive approach does not necessarily translate into the use of more supportive techniques. It is the quantity of the interventions, not the type, that is of importance.

With psychotic patients, especially those who are withdrawn, isolated, and apathetic, an active approach is necessary. Such an approach is helpful in activating the patient to use the sessions more productively It is also useful in addressing those areas of ego weakness that are avoided by the patient.

32. What Is the Mechanism of Change in Psychotherapy?

There are two main mechanisms of change in psychotherapy: change via insight and change via the relationship. The first mechanism emphasizes interventions, particularly insight-oriented ones. The second emphasizes identification and internalization. Regarding the latter, change does not occur by any specific role played by the therapist; it takes place silently as the therapy unfolds in its natural way. Insight plays a larger role in psychotherapy with "healthier" patients; the relationship assumes greater importance with more "troubled" individuals. Yet, both of these mechanisms play important roles with all patients.

CHAPTER

The Office Setting

33. How Important Is the Office Setting?

The office setting is overrated; an ideal environment certainly is not necessary to do effective psychotherapy. It wanes in importance in comparison with the expertise, experience, and personal characteristics of the therapist. Yet, it is important for both the patient and the therapist to be reasonably comfortable with their place of work. A certain amount of comfort contributes to one's own esteem, thus enhancing effective psychotherapy.

34. What Factors Are Important in Setting Up an Office?

The office should be big enough to hold three chairs, reasonably spaced; a psychoanalytic couch (if one is a psychoanalyst); and possibly a desk. Three chairs are needed, even if one does individual work only, because there are occasional meetings with family members and significant others. If one does family or group work, obviously the room and furnishings need to be expanded. The chairs for both the therapist and the patient should be comfortable, with good back supports. It is helpful if they are identical; some patients feel insulted and devalued if the therapist has a more desirable chair. A desk is useful for paperwork but should not be used in therapy sessions because it contributes to an authoritarian atmosphere, clearly distinguishing the patient from the therapist.

Tissues are a useful adjunct, both contributing an appropriate supportive element and providing another vehicle through which the therapist can learn about the patient. A clock, best placed in a position that can be easily viewed by the therapist but not the patient, is needed if one is to start and end sessions on time. Ashtrays used to be routine but now are hardly permissible. Even if the therapist does not object to smoking, he or she can be certain that, in the current culture, many patients will.

An office that transmits a feeling of warmth is desirable. With that in mind, artwork, books, plants, carpeting, and other decorations reflective of the therapist's taste are reasonable. Very personal items such as family pictures, however, are to be avoided. These items have the potential to interfere with the therapy, serving either as impediments to the elaboration and resolution of transference or as objects of jealousy and envy. More important than the office decor is consistency. Thus, especially when one is dealing with more disturbed patients, decorating changes should be minimized.

Extraneous outside noises, of course, should be kept to a minimum whenever possible. However, one can learn from deviations even here. When I had to suffer through loud construction noises outside my office, the variance in tolerance from one patient to another was remarkable. Some patients acted as if there were no problem whatsoever as we both shouted, while others threatened to discontinue the therapy until the noise subsided.

35. What About the Waiting Room?

There needs to be a waiting room with several reasonably comfortable chairs and several well-chosen magazines. The traditional psychoanalytic waiting room, constructed in such a way that patients following one another do not see each other, may be ideal but certainly is not necessary. The rationale of that setting inevitably is undone when a patient is slightly late and "bumps into" an earlier patient on the street or in the hall. Reasonable soundproofing from the office is indicated; in my experience, however, no matter what one does, it will not be perfect. Appropriately placed radios and white noise machines can usually remedy problems in this area. Patients look to furnishings and to magazines to get hints, both accurate and distorted, about the therapist. When I first started to subscribe to *New York Magazine*, one of my patients said, "Well, that confirms it. You're a money grabbing, New York Jew!"

36. What About the Bathroom?

A bathroom is obviously needed for the comfort of both the patient and the therapist. It can often lead to interesting material. For example, a patient may leave the bathroom door open, rummage through the closets, or feel obligated to change the toilet paper.

37. What About a Telephone?

There needs to be a phone in the office, at least for outgoing calls. Ideally, neither patient nor therapist will have any awareness of incoming calls. If the phone rings, or if there is a sound indicating an incoming call, the therapist should not answer. A number of therapists, sometimes noting the possibility of an emergency, take incoming calls during sessions. I really do not think that such intrusions can be justified. If one has patients requiring instantaneous attention, alternate methods for dealing with emergencies need to be made. Obviously one has time to check messages and return calls between therapy sessions.

38. Is a Home Office Desirable?

Regarding home offices, they seem quite reasonable. They should be sufficiently separate from the rest of the house to protect the patient from family intrusions, and vice versa. Obviously the patient learns more about the therapist by seeing his or her home, and the therapist needs to be prepared for comments about everything conceivable regarding the surroundings. Theoretically, a home office could detract from transference; practically, I have not found this to be a problem. The one difficulty I have encountered involved a very intrusive narcissistic patient who had difficulty differentiating the office from the rest of the house. Limit setting was needed on several occasions to prevent this patient from wandering throughout the house.

The Initial Interview

39. What Should the Therapist Say When the Patient First Calls?

The first contact with the patient is invariably by phone. This contact can vary from simply setting up an initial appointment to a prolonged discussion. Regarding questions, the therapist can easily answer items regarding fees, office location, time availability, and experience and credentials. Questions regarding the therapist's comfort and expertise with certain types of problems, in addition to the type of therapy typically used, are also reasonable. It is usually advantageous for the therapist to be friendly and open, answering any "relevant" questions in a straightforward manner. It is not advantageous at this early time to delve into the reasons for the questions, to speculate on the dynamics, or to make any kind of interpretive comments. At this stage, these types of interventions appear intrusive and are usually not appreciated. If the questions become more personal or go on and on, limits need to be set, but in a very tactful way. Phone calls resembling initial sessions are best avoided. Contrary to the expectations of some, lengthy phone conversations do not necessarily lead to the patient undergoing treatment with the therapist. In fact, there is probably a positive correlation between minimal phone questions and the referral working out. There is no rule of thumb about the outer limits of preliminary calls. Although it is rarely advantageous to talk more than 15 to 20 minutes, there are exceptions.

At times, the therapist has only 5 or 10 minutes available when he returns the call; if so, it is reasonable to state this at the beginning of the conversation. Sometimes it is appropriate to call the patient back if additional information is desired. The patient can be given a choice.

Therapist: I want to mention that I have an appointment in 10 minutes. If we don't finish by then, I'll be happy to call you back.

Then, after 7 minutes:

Therapist: We are going to have to stop in a minute or two. If you like, we could set up an appointment, or I'd be happy to call you back if you need more information

Sometimes patients inquire what they should expect from the consultation. They are interested in the length of the consultation, what they will be asked, and what types of recommendations the therapist might provide. I explain that I usually take two to three sessions to hear their reasons for coming to see me and to ask questions about their concerns, life, and history. I sometimes add that I might be able to give some preliminary impressions near the end of the first session but that it is usually best to hold off on definitive recommendations until later.

40. What Kinds of Patients Tend to Stay on the Phone, and How Does the Therapist Deal with Them?

Long initial phone questioning is most characteristic of borderline patients. Some of these individuals are preoccupied with searches for the "ideal" therapist. Feeling quite vulnerable to the vicissitudes of relationships, they want to feel as comfortable as possible before the initial session. These patients sometimes look for therapists with whom they feel the right "vibrations, wavelengths, or sensations," the ones they sense are similar to themselves and the ones who share similar values, philosophies, and upbringings. Initial phone conversations can be reflective of these searches. With these individuals, tact and patience are of the greatest importance. Limits have to be set but with the utmost skill and sensitivity.

The following comment was made by a therapist after a 20-minute conversation in which the patient had basically found out all of the necessary information and more: "I don't want to be impolite, but I do have to go in several minutes. I do think we've covered the relevant questions about psychotherapy. Certainly I will be happy to answer additional questions when we meet. Would you like to set up an appointment?"

I was once referred a patient who, I was told, was a difficult and challenging individual. I was further told that this patient was having problems finding a therapist and would welcome working with me. When the patient called, she asked if I would mind answering a few questions before our initial appointment The "few" questions took 35 minutes, and the call was ended by me in a sensitive and polite manner. The call had been cordial, and the patient seemed pleased. She insisted on sending me a number of documents about herself so that she would not have to waste time in the initial session. A large packet arrived by messenger, including the patient's resume, her medical history, various job performances, and a note thanking me for talking with her on the phone and confirming our appointment. The patient arrived at the first appointment with additional questions. I went along and answered all of her questions. I thought that my answers were quite relevant and useful, yet I noticed that the patient did not seem to be "listening" to what I was saying. Instead, she was rushing to the next question. Near the end of the session, I asked her what she thought about therapy at this point. She said she didn't think she wanted to see me. I was a nice man, but I was too old, and she was sick and tired of seeing Jewish therapists anyway. I reviewed my ideas about why pursuing treatment with me seemed advantageous and said that I would be available if she was interested.

Although I had been as open and flexible as possible, in addition to spending an unusual amount of preliminary time, this patient never called back. Despite my being so accommodating, and despite my being highly recommended, she summarily rejected me. Despite what on the surface appeared to be an organized way of evaluating me, she rejected me without reflection or thought.

Another patient, after talking to me briefly on the phone and setting up an appointment, called back and canceled, quite upset about my being Jewish. He called the referring psychiatrist, who greatly encouraged him to give it a try with me.

With that recommendation, the patient called back, set up an appointment, and began a number of years of very productive therapy. This patient had panicked about something that had specific idiosyncratic importance to him. He initially acted under the influence of the panic but was quickly able to undo his actions when, with the help of the referring psychiatrist, he reverted to his usual reflective style. The first patient, in contrast, was uninfluenced by any suggestion, preferring to use her intuition and feelings alone to make her decision.

41. What Are the Goals of the Initial Session?

The ideal initial interview ends with the therapist having some preliminary understanding as to why the patient is seeking help and some beginning knowledge of the patient's personality, conflicts, motivation, and strengths and weaknesses. Of even more importance is the establishment of enough rapport so that the patient is inclined to continue the consultation.

42. How Is the Initial Session Structured?

Upon meeting the patient, I introduce myself, tell her or him to come in, and then say, "Why don't you have a seat there."

I then pause, allowing the patient to take the lead. If the patient asks for clarification about how to begin, I say, "Why don't you tell me about yourself, especially in reference to coming to see me today." I want patients to present their story in their own way; thus, I do not interrupt, except to ask relevant clarifications. I am not concerned about obtaining all of the details in the first session; rather, I am interested in hearing how patients talk and think and in learning about their personality, conflicts, strengths, and weaknesses. I want them to feel as comfortable as possible so that they will continue the process. With that in mind, I make empathic comments whenever relevant and try to maintain a friendly and interested stance.

If the patient's anxiety demands that I ask questions, I do so. Otherwise, I let patients tell their story as they wish. I am particularly interested in their motivation for therapy. With that in mind, sometime during the initial interview (usually during the latter part of the session), I ask their specific ideas about treatment. If they say that they think they are interested in psychotherapy, I ask them how they think that process might work. I might even ask their ideas about the frequency of sessions and what time frame they have in mind.

The 15-Minute Warning

With about 15 minutes left in the session, I note that the session will soon end and that I want to shift the focus. I state that, although what the patient is saying is very important, I want to make sure that she or he has time to ask me any questions that she or he might have. I find it rather important to make this intervention, because many patients have definite questions they "need" to ask. However, they typically do not ask unless invited to do so, at least not until the end of the hour. Then either the session has to be extended or the patient leaves quite frustrated.

In the second session, I always allow the patient to start spontaneously. If the patient looks to me to begin, I often ask what thoughts she or he has had about coming to see me since the first session. If that question does not come up at the beginning, I usually work it into the session later because it often provides an initial indication of the patient's acceptance or rejection of therapy.

43. How Does the Therapist Proceed with History Taking?

After the patient makes her or his initial presentation, and after following this up with relevant questions, I usually move on to a history of previous therapy. Details of past therapy, particularly in terms of problems regarding that therapy, can be quite illuminating to the current treatment, especially with the tendency of so many patients to repeat patterns with previous therapists. Exploration here can lead to discussions about whether and under what circumstances past disruptive patterns might recur.

After this exploration, I move on to take somewhat of a standard history, beginning by stating that it would be helpful to have an outline of the patient's life, starting as early as she or he can remember. I ask relevant questions to learn about the patient's early years and his or her relationship with parents, siblings, and significant others. The history also focuses on how patients viewed themselves in their early years, along with their interests, friends, and problem areas. A discussion of how they reacted to going to school and a history of their school years follows, with reference to how they did academically and how they got along with students and teachers. This merges into a work history with analogous emphases on how the patient performed and how she or he related to peers and supervisors. A sexual history is tactfully included.

Throughout the history taking, the patient's uneasiness, defenses, awkwardness, and reluctance to share certain information need to be respected. As noted, a complete history is not necessary at this time; details can be filled in later. There is great variability from patient to patient regarding the completeness of the initial history. This relates to the ease with which the patient is able to talk and to delve into sensitive areas. Initial history taking usually involves two to three sessions, although more time may be useful when evaluating for psychoanalysis. At the conclusion of this process, the therapist makes recommendations.

For most patients, the history-taking process can proceed as outlined. However, a number of patients (most of whom are in the borderline grouping) present themselves in some state of crisis or regression. These individuals are preoccupied with their problems and want to address them as soon as possible. They have little tolerance or interest in giving a detailed history. For this type of patient, history taking needs to be abbreviated until more pressing issues have been addressed and until the patient is in a calmer state. For some patients, a good history is not obtained until late in the treatment.

44. How Are Recommendations Made?

Recommendations need to correspond at least somewhat to the patient's way of thinking. Thus, if the patient is more comfortable with the term *counseling* than with the term *therapy*, it is advantageous to continue with the former. Of course, it is always advisable to explore exactly what patients mean by *counseling*, as with any term they use. Because many patients are fearful about a long-term commitment, it is best not to be too enthusiastic about this aspect of psychotherapy. Unfortunately I have scared a number of patients away by noting, when asked, that several years seemed to be a reasonable estimate in terms of therapy duration. It is better to say, "We will be in a better position to judge as the therapy progresses."

In presenting recommendations, it is useful to cite specifics of the patient's problems that led to the recommendations. In patients for whom medication is a consideration, the pros and cons of medication, psychotherapy, or both can be enumerated. Feedback from the patient is useful as the recommendations are spelled out. Several examples of recommendations follow. The first three examples do not address the patient's specific problems. The fourth and fifth examples do.

Example 1

Therapist: You've clearly spelled out the reasons for coming here, and you've presented a very nice outline of your life. I think I can make some recommendations at this point. What do you think?

Patient: That's fine. Go ahead.

Therapist: It sounds to me that coming in on a regular basis to talk about your problems would make sense.

Patient: That's what I thought. How often do I need to come?

Therapist (taking into account the limited financial situation and the patient's already-stated preference): We could start with weekly sessions and see how that goes.

Patient: Fine.

Example 2

Therapist: At this point, I think I have a good idea about why you've come to see me. And I do agree with you that psychotherapy makes eminent sense.

Patient: I've been putting it off for years. I'm really glad I've come. How often should we meet?

Therapist: What are your ideas?

Patient: I really think twice a week would be best. But I'm not sure if I can afford it.

Therapist: I agree that twice a week makes sense. Let's talk about the finances more, to see if we can arrange it.

Example 3

Therapist: I think I have a good idea about your reasons for coming to see me. Where do you want to go from here?

Patient: I'm not really clear. I really hate these depressed symptoms and would like to get rid of them as fast as possible. A number of my friends have been helped by Zoloft.

Therapist: We certainly could give Zoloft, or a different antidepressant, a trial. Let me take a few minutes to outline the pros and cons of medication versus psychotherapy in regard to the symptoms you present. *(The therapist then elaborates, concluding that an antidepressant is reasonable but that talking about the problems also makes sense.)*

Patient: To tell you the truth, what I really want is to get rid of the depression. If I can do that with medication, and I feel better, I probably won't want to come in regularly. But I'm willing to come for a few more sessions.

Sometimes the patient asks whether the therapy will be of definitive help. After exploring her or his ideas, I often state that although there are no guarantees, I think the therapy should be useful. I emphasize that it certainly will not be harmful. I try to be specific about how therapy might be beneficial in relation to presenting problems.

Example 4

Therapist: You have presented a history of having a number of relationships with a number of different men. Often you hope that the relationship will evolve into something lasting, but it doesn't. You don't understand why but are beginning to think that this pattern has something to do with you. I think that it would be reasonable to expect that psychotherapy will help you to develop a better understanding of what goes on here. In fact, it would be reasonable for this understanding to help you alter this pattern.

Example 5

Therapist: You describe a history of a number of discrete episodes of depression. The episodes are never disabling but can be very bothersome. They usually are related to criticisms by peers or supervisors. They begin when you feel criticized and end when you feel more accepted. To answer your question, it is possible that an antidepressant would be helpful in altering this pattern. Yet, the episodes are very short-lived and totally related to how you feel you are being treated by others. Psychotherapy should be useful in helping you understand the way you respond to other people. It is possible that you could alter the pattern by therapy alone.

45. What Is the Best Way to Refer to Another Therapist?

The patient does not always enter treatment with the evaluating therapist. Sometimes the evaluation is structured in such a way that the evaluator is excluded as a possible therapist. At other times, there might be some initial discomfort with the evaluator, geographical and/or financial factors might play a role, or the patient might favor a therapist of a specific sex or of a specific ethnic group.

When making a referral, a common practice is to give patients three names so that they can interview these individuals and make their own selection. I do not agree with this approach. I do not know how a patient can make a rational decision about which of three therapists, often similarly trained, will ultimately be best for him or her on the basis of one or two interviews. The decision is likely to be made in terms of initial comfort level or superficial items that do not correlate with ultimate success.

When making a referral, I prefer to provide only one name. I tell patients that, although I think the therapist selected should work out for them, they should call me if there are any problems. Before providing the name, I discuss with the patient the type of therapist she or he desires, along with finances, geographical location, and any other relevant issues. With that information in mind, I select a therapist I clearly think will work. In addition, I find out whether the therapist has hours available that are suitable for the patient and whether he or she is willing to see the patient. If the patient is dissatisfied with the referral, I am willing to discuss the relevant details with the patient, making another referral when appropriate. One name, given in this manner, works out the vast majority of the time. If, however, patients are insistent on getting three names, I comply with their wishes.

CHAPTER

Arrangements

46. What Initial Arrangements Need to Be Discussed with the Patient?

Arrangements regarding psychotherapy need to be discussed and established as early as possible. These arrangements include scheduling of times, payments, missed appointments, guidelines for the patient, and, on occasion, expectations regarding interactions between therapist and patient outside the sessions.

Some patients enter treatment with a certain amount of urgency, in a state of crisis or regression. They are preoccupied with their problems and want to address them as soon as possible. For these patients, discussion of the arrangements can be burdensome, seeming like a distraction. For patients in this category, I discuss the arrangements piecemeal, after some of the presenting issues have been addressed and the patient is in a calmer state. The patient is then able to approach the arrangements with both more interest and more cooperation.

47. What About Scheduling?

Scheduling times convenient for both the patient and the therapist is, of course, ideal. From the therapist's perspective, the sessions need to start on time and end on time. From the patient's perspective, they will, it is hoped, start on time; however, whether they do or do not, they need to end on time. The ability and responsibility of managing time is integral to a structured and stable life. Adhering to time agreements conforms with the realities of life in general. Thus, except in clear emergencies, there should be no deviations regarding extending the sessions.

48. What About the Frequency of Sessions?

When doing analytically oriented psychotherapy, the rule of thumb is that more sessions are better. Frequent sessions produce intensity and momentum, providing a forum where the transference can most easily be elaborated and worked through. The "usual" is twice a week, but more frequent sessions can often be helpful. Although some consider once a week insufficient, I find that selected patients can do analytically oriented work effectively with this "minimal" frequency. Often, both therapist and patient notice a significant difference when increasing from once to twice a week; the difference is not as striking when going from two to three times a week.

Regarding more supportive psychotherapy, once a week for "reasonably stable" patients is often sufficient. More frequent sessions are needed for "unstable" patients, who are having acute difficulty with some of their basic ego functions. When these patients stabilize, weekly sessions can often be resumed. As noted previously, the principle underlying the number of sessions is the opposite when comparing analytically oriented to more supportive psychotherapy. For the former, increased sessions are used to promote intensity; for the latter they are used to decrease intensity and stop regression.

49. What About the Spacing of Sessions?

Regarding biweekly psychotherapy, most therapists space sessions with one or two days between meetings. This type of spacing minimizes waiting "too long" for the next session and decreases anxiety in those patients who "need" to talk to their therapists about current feelings and events. However, with selected patients, sessions on consecutive days can be advantageous. Sessions spaced in that way enhance focus (especially in the second meeting) on the intraphysic and the internal rather than the external. The rule of thumb is that the more time between sessions, the more the tendency to focus on external events. More supportive therapy lends itself to maximum spacing. Although insight-oriented work can sometimes benefit by consecutive sessions, frequency here is a more important factor than spacing. Although it is important that therapist and patient are comfortable with the spacing, both often can easily adjust to a variety of arrangements.

50. How Are Fees Established?

Payment arrangements need to be addressed early, including both fee and collection policy. Many therapists have flexibility in their fees, with some ability to make adjustments in accordance with the patient's income. In these situations, frank discussion of the patient's finances and insurance coverage needs to be part of fee setting. It is important that both therapist and patient are comfortable with the fee. Therapists need to understand their own financial requirements, including under what circumstances they are willing to accept lower payments. Some patients will volunteer to pay more than they can reasonably afford. Because this situation can rapidly undermine the treatment, it needs to be avoided. On the other hand, some patients try to pay as little as possible. A fee clearly too low can be indicative of a sense of entitlement and/or devaluation of the treatment. In cases of reduced fees, it is always good policy to allow for periodic reevaluations.

A usual practice is to bill at the end of the month and collect shortly thereafter. Payment can be due the session after the bill, 2 weeks later, or a month later. Sometimes there is an agreement to wait until the patient has collected from her or his insurance. In this case, a reasonable policy is for payment to be provided in a prescribed length of time (for example, 1 month) or when the insurance check arrives, whichever is first. This puts responsibility on the patient to send the bill in on time, call the insurance company when necessary, and so forth. Whatever the arrangements, they need to be clearly agreed upon. Deviations from the agreement then can be discussed in the treatment hours, as they occur.

51. Should Patients Be Charged for Missed Appointments?

Not long ago, the usual rule regarding missed appointments was for the therapist to charge unless he or she filled the time. A reasonable contingency was that, given advance notice, the therapist was willing to reschedule if possible. Although still reasonable in many cases, this rule appears to be losing favor. Some therapists have a rather liberal policy of not charging if notice is given a certain number of hours (for example, 24 or 72) in advance. Others do not charge if there is a good reason for the missed appointment. The latter is never a good idea. Illness, car problems, college examinations, or other important appointments, although reasonable on the surface, are often used as resistance. Evaluation of the reasons puts the therapist in the unwanted position of an authority figure, inviting the patient to rebel.

From patient to patient variations in terms of missing appointments are truly amazing. I have seen a number of patients who have never missed a session over a number of years of multiple sessions per week. Other patients miss regularly (several times a month), for reasons they feel are totally unavoidable and beyond their control. I have seen several patients who missed appointments for very minor illnesses, acting as if this practice were totally reasonable and the norm. In these cases, the missed appointments were related to patient self-concepts that were quite fragile and also somewhat entitled. In the course of therapy, these images were able to be addressed and eventually modified. Regarding patients who never miss appointments, occasional absences late in the therapy can be a positive sign, reflecting the relaxation of overactive superegos.

Therapists can show some flexibility in establishing agreements regarding missed sessions. I favor telling the patient that my usual policy is to charge for missed sessions unless I fill the time, with the exception that I am willing to reschedule hours, if possible, when given advance notice. I explain to patients that I understand that whereas many understand such a policy, others have difficulty with it. Thus, if the patient has any misgivings about the policy, I am willing to discuss them. I do believe that the policy, as stated, is beyond the usual experience of many, making it difficult for them to understand. Some patients see the policy as overly rigid, greedy, one-sided, and unfair. With those who are not able to understand the policy from the therapist's perspective, the policy is not a good one. In these cases, modifications are necessary. With some patients in whom I sense that there will be clear antipathy toward the usual policy, I do not bring it up. If and when a problem arises, I approach it in a flexible manner.

The following vignette represents the most extreme situation in my experience regarding the policy of paying for missed sessions. Therapy with Ms. C seemed off to an uneventful start, that is, until the fifth week or so. Earlier on I had told Ms. C that my usual policy was to charge for missed sessions unless I could fill the time. I had said that I would be willing to discuss this policy if she had any misgivings about it, with the clear implication that there was flexibility for change. When Ms. C offered no objections, we moved on. Then, around the fifth week, Ms. C said that she had been thinking about my fee policy and that, in fact, she had become increasingly obsessed about it. Her conclusion was that it was totally unacceptable. After considerable discussion, I said that although I had originally felt that the policy was reasonable, I could understand her objections; furthermore, I told her that, as a result of these objections, the policy would not apply to her. This, however, did not eliminate the issue. The fee policy became the main topic, session after session. Despite our detailed discussions, Ms. C became of the opinion that although the fee policy would not apply to her, it was nevertheless clear evidence that I was insensitive, unconcerned, inclined to treat her unfairly, and interested only in money. She thought it would be difficult to work with such a self-centered, unempathic, money-oriented individual. With the accumulation of other evidence of my lack of concern and insensitivity, such as my letting her in a minute late on one occasion, my taking a week's vacation, and my occasionally moving about in a restless way, Ms. C concluded that it would be absolutely useless to continue treatment with me. After exploration of this issue, I referred her to a colleague.

Regarding another patient, I had to use some quick thinking regarding the fee policy. In this case, after a lengthy evaluation and after a thorough discussion of the guidelines regarding psychotherapy, including the fee policy, the patient said that he was ready to begin treatment. He entered the next session saying that although he was ready to begin, he refused to pay for missed sessions in instances in which he gave me reasonable notice. Thinking as fast as I could, I suggested a modification of my usual fee policy: when the patient gave me advanced cancellation notice, the responsibility would fall on him to determine whether the cancellation was reasonable and whether he should pay for the session. This agreement would be subject to review and revision by either of us. In this highly conscientious and motivated patient, this modification never became a practical problem. Actually, it enabled the patient's conflicts regarding the fee policy to easily enter into the treatment hours.

52. What Guidelines Is the Patient Given?

It is useful for the patient to be given a set of guidelines regarding psychotherapy near the initiation of treatment. These guidelines are similar to the basic "rule" of analysis, but with modifications applicable to psychotherapy. Similar to the basic "rule" of analysis, they establish a frame for the therapy that can be returned to whenever there is a deviation. Like Gray (1994), I do not present the guidelines as instructions or rules, finding that too authoritarian and rigid. It is puzzling to me that although these guidelines are standard for psychoanalysis, few therapists spell them out for psychotherapy. Kernberg (Kernberg, Seltzer, Koenigsberg, Carr, & Appelbaum, 1989) is one clear exception.

A standard therapist presentation that is useful for most patients is as follows: "The sessions are yours, to talk about anything you want. It will be up to you to choose the topics. Often there will be topics that are on your mind that you very much want to talk about. At other times, this will be less clear. At times when you do not have topics of pressing importance, it is helpful to talk freely about anything that comes to mind. In fact, whenever you have extraneous thoughts or fantasies, it is useful to talk about them. There are certain thoughts that some people find difficult to talk about and are tempted to omit. I want to urge you to do your best not to omit those types of thoughts. These include thoughts that cause uncomfortable feelings, such as anxiety, anger, embarrassment, or shame; ones that you view as silly or irrelevant; ones that you are fearful that I will disapprove of; and any thoughts, positive or negative, that refer to the therapy or to me personally."

As noted, once the guidelines are established, they become useful reference points to return to whenever there is a deviation. Thus, if a patient, after a month or so, says nothing about the therapy, the therapist might make the following comment: "I want to bring up one item. When we started therapy, I mentioned that one of the things that would be useful to hear about was any thoughts that you had, either positive or negative, about the therapy or about me. You haven't said anything about that, and I was wondering about your thoughts on that topic." As a discussion of this topic unfolds, the therapist might inquire about what inhibited the patient from bringing it up herself or himself.

53. Are Contracts Desirable?

Regarding arrangements at the outset of psychotherapy, I find those just enumerated—scheduling of times, payments, missed appointments, and guidelines for the patient—more than adequate. They provide a useful frame for the treatment and are usually not too cumbersome or detailed for the patient. Longer and more specific contractual agreements, if needed, are often best initiated later in the therapy, at a time when the patient is more enthusiastic about dealing with them and when the therapist has a better understanding of the patient's dynamics. Obvious exceptions occur when problems are introduced immediately and are of a nature that demand rapid attention. Problems of this nature include overt suicidal tendencies and any acting out that might rapidly undermine the therapy. Chronic, less dangerous forms of acting out can be addressed later, as they enter the therapy hours spontaneously. The technique of pointing out specific negative experiences in past therapies and the possibility of their recurrence in the current therapy is a good early intervention. However, it need not be part of a contract.

Contracts can provide a false sense of security to the therapist. They have little validity without a reasonable therapeutic alliance, and this alliance is often lacking in the early phases of treatment. It does little good to set up agreements if patients are to ignore them as soon as they are in a different frame of mind. Unfortunately, this is the case with many borderline patients, whose moods shift rapidly. At the time the contract is agreed upon, patients might fully believe that they will, without fail, call the therapist or go to the emergency room if they feel actively suicidal.

Then, when they are actually overcome with strong suicidal feelings, the contract loses its meaning. This is not to say that contracts with suicidal patients should not be initiated; in fact, they should. They sometimes are useful early on, and they often become more effective with time, as the therapeutic alliance is strengthened.

When using a contract, the therapist should never set up agreements that he or she is apt to negate. I have heard examples of contractual agreements to terminate treatment after suicide attempts. Then, after the attempts, the therapist feels differently and continues the work. Basically, I would never set up a contract for which the consequence is termination. Likewise, therapists should not set up agreements in which the patient is required to forgo behavior that is related to his or her core psychopathology. The patient is unable to keep such an agreement. The principle here is simple. All individuals have tendencies and propensities to certain symptoms, certain forms of acting out, and certain behavioral patterns. No matter what they are, they recur under stress. Only through a thorough understanding of the stresses involved in psychotherapy or through elimination of such stresses in the real world can the symptoms and behavior patterns end.

It should be noted that others have a decidedly different viewpoint regarding contracts, especially when working with more disturbed patients. Some (Kernberg et al., 1989; Rockland, 1992; Yeomans, Selzer, & Clarin, 1992) place great emphasis in this area, at times structuring the therapy around the contract.

54. Should Smoking and Food Be Allowed During the Sessions?

In the current culture, it is best to prohibit smoking during the sessions. The reason is not that the therapist objects to the patient's alleviating his or her anxiety in this way; nor is this prohibition based on health reasons. Rather, it is related to the current general disdain for smoking among a fair portion of the population. Even if smoking does not bother the therapist, smoke from previous sessions will certainly offend a number of patients. Thus, if a patient asks about smoking, I explain that although I do not find it overly objectionable, so many object to smoke in the room that I have made the office a nonsmoking area.

Regarding food and drinks, I do not prohibit them. Certain orally oriented patients invariably bring one or the other to the session. Although some therapists do not allow food and drinks for fear of damage to the room, I have never had that problem. Discussion of the dynamics of the eating and drinking is best left until later in the therapy.

The drinking of alcohol is obviously not desirable during session hours. Except under extenuating circumstances, it is a bad idea to go through with a session if the patient has recently been drinking. Alcohol can alter thought processes, judgment, and impulse control in ways that inhibit reasonable psychotherapy.

55. What About Interactions Between Therapist and Patient Outside of the Sessions?

Regarding interactions between the patient and the therapist outside the therapy hours, the general rule is the fewer, the better. Therapists can make it clear that they welcome and even expect calls at times of true emergency; otherwise, they neither expect nor desire them. Emergencies necessitating calls sometimes need to be spelled out; many so-called "emergencies" can be easily handled without the therapist. The generalization here is that psychotherapy proceeds best when it is confined to the therapy sessions. If there is not enough time during the sessions, the frequency of the sessions can be increased. In addition, extra appointments can be scheduled in accordance with the patient's desires and "needs." There are numerous exceptions. Some patients, for example, need very brief occasional contact to confirm the reality of the therapist. Others need various kinds of brief contact to avoid overwhelming anxiety. Under these circumstances, the therapist and patient can arrange limited telephone conversations.

Specific agreements regarding phone calls need not come up at the beginning of treatment, unless an obvious problem is anticipated. Discussion can wait until after the first or even second phone call. At that time, the rationale for limits can be stated and discussed. Firm limits set in a reasonable way can make the difference between virtually no phone calls and daily phone calls. To set these limits well, therapists need to have solid boundaries regarding the therapy hours themselves, along with the belief and experience that therapy is best carried out when it is confined to well-defined sessions.

Transference and the Therapeutic Alliance

56. What Is the Difference Between the Therapeutic Alliance and Transference?

The therapeutic alliance is the collaborative relationship between the patient and the therapist, established to facilitate the work of psychotherapy. It demands that the patient maintain an observing ego that continually focuses on the therapeutic process. This observing ego is in alliance with the therapist against the patient's conflicts and resistances. Although it can include unconscious components, the therapeutic alliance operates mainly on a conscious level. In contrast, transference is an unconscious process in which the patient displaces or "transfers" onto the therapist feelings and thoughts originally directed toward the important people of the patient's early childhood. Transference includes not only these feelings and thoughts but also defenses against them. It is based on both the actual and fantasized past, as experienced by the patient.

The concept of transference just outlined is that of the classical school. This is in contrast to a more contemporary version, especially influenced by the relational school. In this version the transference is seen as a joint creation between patient and therapist. The therapist, like the patient, is viewed as a unique individual, with his own theory of how therapy works, his own personality, his own conflicts, his own strengths and weaknesses, his own idiosyncrasies, and his own countertransference. All these factors relating to the therapist, like analogous ones of the patient, influence the transference. Thus the transference is thought to be jointly created or jointly constructed between patient and therapist.

57. What Patients Have Problems Forming a Therapeutic Alliance?

Borderline patients and psychotic patients with paranoid features have the most problems in forming and maintaining therapeutic alliances. Some narcissistic patients experience more subtle difficulties. In marked contrast is the neurotic patient, for whom a strong therapeutic alliance is basically a given. Patients who have difficulties here often have had childhoods in which there were inconsistent, unstable, and unreliable figures to trust and with whom to identify. When there are alliance problems, these problems must be addressed vigorously and repetitively. Except for certain emergency situations, such problems take precedence over other issues.

58. How Is a Weak Therapeutic Alliance Strengthened?

A weak alliance is strengthened gradually, without specific interventions, in relation to factors regarding the stability of the therapeutic environment. Thus, the alliance is strengthened as the patient experiences the therapist over time as being stable, competent, consistent, reliable, conscientious, and concerned. In addition to these nonspecific factors, so crucial over time, the therapist must actively intervene whenever there are overt problems with the alliance.

Whenever there is a disruption in the alliance, the therapist needs to point this out to the patient, as well as invite the patient to explore the difficulty. Disruptions in the alliance need to be addressed throughout the therapy, whenever they occur. The therapist might make a comment similar to the following: "There seems to be a problem with the two of us working together effectively. Do you agree? I wonder if there is something I am saying or doing that is contributing? Could we talk about that?"

In the early stages of therapy, when one is eliciting the cooperation of the patient, it is helpful to place the responsibility for the disruption on the therapist. Later, as the alliance becomes progressively strengthened, more responsibility can be placed on the patient. Continuing with the preceding example, the patient might respond: "Actually, now that you mention it, I am bothered by the way you keep turning the air conditioner off and on. When I say it, it sounds silly. I know you're trying to get the temperature right. Yet it bothers me. Also, I hate it when you move around in the chair. You don't do it so much, yet it's still annoying."

Here the patient focuses on surface complaints about the therapist. A response early in treatment should stay on the same level, as follows: "I'm sorry that what I do is bothersome. As you've already guessed, there isn't a thermostat here, and you're right about my moving about. I'll try to refrain from that as much as possible, and I will also try to stop playing with the air conditioner. I'm glad you were able to bring this up. Let me know if this again becomes annoying. For that matter, please tell me anything that bothers you here."

Only later in the treatment are factors within the patient that contribute to the alliance focused on and explored. An example taken from a patient in therapy for a number of years is as follows: "The problem with you is that you don't listen to me and empathize with me. You're more interested in some little detail. And I find that so infuriating! All I want you to do is to listen and to be empathic. Is that asking too much?"

In response, the therapist first notes that he does not want to sound defensive but that he thought he was listening. He also was trying to be empathic. He does understand that it can be annoying when he focuses on a detail rather than on how the patient feels. He then goes on to explain why he focused on the particular detail. The patient is satisfied with his explanation, and patient and therapist are able to explore the detail at length. After this, the therapist returns to the patient's sensitivity about his "not listening and being empathic." The patient is now able to explore her early childhood, during which her parents did not listen empathically and were more interested in the details of their own lives than in being in tune with their daughter.

In this example, there was a temporary disruption in the therapeutic alliance based on what the patient perceived as a lack of empathy. Here the therapist was able to address the disruption, regain a reasonable therapeutic alliance, and then help the patient to focus on her role in the disruption. Repetitive occurrences of the preceding type of interaction, with recurrent clarification and focus on the patient's sensitivities as a child, now being played out in the transference, were met with both a gradual lessening of these sensitivities in the patient and a continued strengthening of the alliance.

59. With What Patients Does Transference Develop Rapidly?

Patients in the borderline grouping typically show a rapid involvement with the therapist and the transference. In fact, the rapid mobilization of transference distinguishes the typical borderline individual from the typical neurotic. Neurotic patients become involved with transference at a slower and more gradual pace, at times with some difficulty. Psychoanalysis provides a forum for these patients that enhances the development of an intense transference. The borderline patient, in contrast, easily focuses on the transference without psychoanalysis. Withdrawn, isolated, and schizoid borderline individuals, for whom rapid transference involvement is not typical, are exceptions.

60. What Are Some Generalizations Regarding the Handling of Transference?

There are several generalizations regarding transference. Whenever possible, the transference should be allowed to unfold and develop without intervention. However, whenever the transference becomes negative and/or interferes with the therapeutic alliance, rapid intervention is necessary. Unexplored negative transferences often lead to unwanted acting out, directly threatening and undermining the therapy. Thus, even subtle indications of negative transference need to be addressed. Positive transferences that are either overtly idealized or overtly eroticized are generally handled in a manner similar to that of negative transferences. In these cases, the speed of the intervention is less important, because destructive acting out does not occur as rapidly No intervention is needed regarding the mildly positive portion of the transference that contributes to the therapeutic alliance. Mild to moderate idealizations can likewise usually be left alone, at least initially

61. How Does the Therapist Deal with Negative Transferences?

Interventions regarding negative transferences can often be confined to some combination of clarification, confrontation, and interpretation. Only when these types of insight-oriented techniques are ineffective are more supportive interventions needed. Details regarding the different types of interventions are provided in Chapter 9, "Basic Strategy."

One of the most difficult types of negative transference is chronic devaluation, sometimes occurring after a referral from a highly idealized previous therapist. I have been the recipient of two referrals of this sort, and neither worked out. One patient devalued me from the moment she walked through the door. The basic complaint was that she found me stupid in comparison with her past therapist. I was surprised by her complaint and told her that I had been criticized for not being empathic or warm enough but never for being stupid. She responded that she found me very warm and that, in fact, she liked me. It just was that I was intellectually dull and, if not stupid, certainly not very bright. This stance was used to devalue virtually anything I said. Of course, I pointed out how difficult it must be to see me after years of work with a therapist she found so brilliant and intuitive. I also wondered whether it might not be difficult for her to see anyone after her former therapist. I pointed out, in a nice way, the possibility of some idealization of her past therapist and some devaluation of me. Despite numerous interventions that I thought were on target, the devaluation continued. Finally, I recommended a transfer to another therapist, and the patient agreed. Parenthetically, this is the only time I have initiated a transfer in circumstances of this sort. It is obviously much better to help the patient work out the problems in the transference.

In the second example, the devaluation was more indirect and more subtle. The patient didn't find the location of the office optimal, and he didn't like the carpet; most of all, however, he didn't like the chair. He felt his chair was positioned lower than mine, connoting that I was superior and he was inferior. Then there was something bothersome about me that he couldn't put his finger on. I noted the latter as something worthwhile to explore. In addition, I focused on the superior-inferior feelings. Again I noted how difficult it must be seeing a new therapist after years of such positive work with another. The patient said he was tempted to leave but didn't want to, because I came so highly recommended. Also, he was unclear why he was so uncomfortable with me. He wanted to explore things more fully, as did I, but he left precipitously.

62. How Does the Therapist Deal with Eroticized Transferences?

Regarding eroticized transferences, when they occur early in the treatment and are mild, they sometimes contribute to a positive attitude toward psychotherapy. Often these transference feelings are unexpressed and innocuous, becoming diminished with time. More overt expressions of eroticized transferences need to be addressed. Subtle hints or overt expressions of sexual acting out between the patient and the therapist are somewhat common in situations involving female therapists and male patients who typically sexualize relationships. A comment by the therapist, such as "It seems easier for you to express your sexual feelings to me than to address the problems that brought you here" or "You seem more comfortable flirting with me than in talking about your problems in forming long-term relationships," is often all that is needed to overcome this type of resistance. In cases in which there are more persistent demands for sexual acting out, a more definitive technique, often including limit setting, is required. If a patient thinks that sex is a real possibility, the reality and rationale for its prohibition need to be discussed.

Two examples of rather striking eroticizations follow. The first involves a borderline patient I had been seeing in intensive psychotherapy for more than a year. One day at the beginning of a session, this patient calmly announced that she was really "horny" and that she wanted to have sex with me. She elaborated both her reasons and the sexual acts she had in mind. I first commented on how this request seemed like a resistance to working on her problems and then elaborated one reason after another why sex would not make sense psychotherapeutically. To each reason I gave, she had a rebuttal. After exhausting every imaginable idea that I could think of, she said, "But it'll only take a few minutes!" Needless to say, there was no acting out.

Another patient, overtly psychotic and undergoing therapy in a hospital setting, rapidly undressed after entering my office. Thinking rapidly, I stated that I would leave the office briefly and that, when I returned, I expected her to be fully clothed. When I returned in 5 minutes, she had complied with the request.

CHAPTER 9

Basic Strategy

63. Is There a Basic Strategy for Psychotherapy?

There are at least two basic strategies for psychotherapy. With the underlying assumption that permanent change is best effected when the patient reexperiences and works through his or her conflicts with the therapist, one strategy attempts to maximize the development and resolution of the transference. Using techniques analogous to those of psychoanalysis, with an emphasis on insight-oriented interventions, the therapist tries to obtain an intense transference. The therapist initially comments on any resistance to the formation of the transference and later helps the patient to understand himself or herself by correlating the transference with both current and childhood relationships. This is the strategy underlying analytically oriented psychotherapy. It is useful with patients who can form an intense transference in the psychotherapy situation without disruptive fragmentation.

A second strategy emphasizes the formation and maintenance of a positive therapeutic alliance and the use of that alliance to explore and gain understanding into the patient's conflicts. The focus is on present-day interactions and relationships and their correlation to the past. This strategy downplays transference as a therapeutic modality. Although transference reactions are noted, especially when they occur as resistances, the elaboration and resolution of the transference does not play a major role. This strategy is particularly useful with patients who cannot form a reasonably intense transference within the psychotherapy situation. It is also used with patients who form extremely intense transferences, with marked tendencies toward undesirable acting out and/or disruptive fragmenta-tion. In addition, it is used by a number of therapists with basically all patients. This is the strategy underlying dynamically oriented psycho-therapy.

The second strategy varies greatly in accordance with the therapist's use of insight-oriented versus supportive techniques. Supportive therapy per se can be considered a subgroup of this strategy, with an emphasis on the latter techniques. Here major goals include supporting and enhanc-ing ego functioning and stemming regression. Sometimes the therapeutic strategy includes combinations of the two basic strategies just enumer-ated, as with patients in the borderline grouping. Details regarding in-sight-oriented versus supportive techniques are provided in Chapter 10, "Therapeutic Interventions."

64. What Strategies Are Recommended for the Different Large Groupings?

For patients in the normal-neurotic grouping who suffer from deep-seated character problems, most obviously manifested in failures in maintaining long-term intimate relationships or in failures in maximizing their poten-tial at work, psychoanalysis is recommended. When psychoanalysis can-not be undertaken with this group, for whatever reason, one must con-sider an alternate strategy. Here there is a difference of opinion. One group of therapists favors a strategy emphasizing transference and simulating psychoanalysis. A second group, influenced by the difficulty many neu-rotic patients experience in forming intense transferences outside of psy-choanalysis, favors a strategy that deemphasizes transference. Still others use a transference-oriented strategy for those neurotics who form intense transferences easily (often these individuals are hysterical in terms of per-sonality type) while favoring a non-transference-oriented approach for those unable to do so (often these individuals are obsessive in terms of personality type). In all cases, insight-oriented techniques are empha-sized.

For patients in the narcissistic grouping, a strategy emphasizing trans-ference is often best. This strategy can take the form of psychoanalysis per se or of an analytically oriented psychotherapy. Some narcissistic patients have difficulty with the formation and development of transference, and thus a non-transference-oriented strategy is preferable. As with the nor-mal-neurotic grouping, insight-oriented techniques are emphasized.

The question of strategy for patients in the borderline grouping is more complex. For this reason, a separate section is devoted to this grouping.

For patients in the psychotic grouping, the treatment of choice involves a strategy focusing on the therapeutic alliance and deemphasizing transference. Here supportive techniques are usually favored. However, even in this grouping, as the patient improves, there can often be a switch to more insight-oriented interventions.

65. What Is the Basic Strategy for Borderline Patients?

Rapid mobilization of the transference is typical of the borderline patient in the early phases of psychotherapy. Taking advantage of this proclivity, one starts therapy with a strategy that focuses on the development and resolution of the transference. However, because of the borderline patients' typical difficulty in maintaining a positive therapeutic alliance and their tendency to form negative transferences, psychotherapy for this group, although analytically oriented, is very different from therapy with patients in the normal-neurotic grouping.

Ideally, the transference is allowed to unfold and develop with little intervention. This ideal is rarely accomplished in the early phases, during which both negative transferences and disruptions to the therapeutic alliance are the norm. Meaningful interventions regarding core difficulties can occur only when there is a workable therapeutic alliance; thus, they should be initiated only when the alliance is reasonable. By interventions regarding core difficulties, I refer to interventions other than those needed to deal with negative transference and disrupted alliance. These latter interventions, of course, also refer to core problems of the patient. Typically, there is an oscillation between focus on the therapeutic alliance and interventions involving other core difficulties. Unending sequences occur, as follows: disruption of the therapeutic alliance leads to focus on the disruption, followed by strengthening of the alliance. This leads to an intervention regarding a core difficulty, which causes another disruption in the therapeutic alliance, with the preceding sequence repeating itself.

As a means of minimizing disruptions, interventions are delivered with an empathic attitude, in an affirmative way, with preparatory comments, and with input from the patient. Details regarding the delivery of these interventions are provided in Chapter 10, "Therapeutic Interventions." With some borderline patients, there are such overwhelming problems in the area of the therapeutic alliance that years of extremely difficult work are required to establish even a tenuous alliance. With these patients, the major focus of the entire therapy can be on alliance issues. More frequently, the alliance becomes gradually but increasingly stable, and the therapeutic focus can shift more and more to interventions regarding other core difficulties. Regarding interventions, insight-oriented techniques are emphasized whenever possible. However, when these techniques are insufficient, they are supplemented or supplanted by more supportive techniques. Whenever reasonable, movement is toward the insight-oriented interventions.

Interestingly enough, although rapid mobilization of transference is typical of the borderline patient in the early phase of psychotherapy, this proclivity sometimes changes after the establishment of a reasonable therapeutic alliance. One group of borderline patients continues to use the transference as the main modality through which their conflicts unfold and are resolved. A second group, after much initial difficulty, maintains a relatively stable therapeutic alliance and then uses that alliance as a vehicle to explore their core difficulties outside of the transference. The focus here is on core difficulties as they play out in the workplace and with spouses, friends, and acquaintances. For this second group, the basic strategy changes from one that emphasizes the transference to one that does not. In other words, one group of borderline patients uses a modified analytically oriented approach throughout the course of psychotherapy. A second group switches from a modified analytically oriented approach to a dynamically oriented strategy after the therapeutic alliance becomes sufficiently stable.

10

CHAPTER

Therapeutic Interventions

66. What Are the Insight-Oriented Interventions?

The interventions of clarification, confrontation, and interpretation are the ones most usually associated with insight-oriented work. Clarification (Bibring, 1954) means to see things in a clearer way. It refers to matters that are conscious or subconscious but not unconscious. Clarification helps the patient to become clearer about feelings, attitudes, thoughts, behavior patterns, and perceptions. The therapist often uses clarification to help the patient bring together contradictory attitudes, behavior, and ideas.

Confrontation is a subcomponent of clarification (Meissner, 1980). Clarification usually appears more neutral on the part of the therapist, whereas confrontation involves a more intrusive stance. Confrontations are sometimes designed to create conflict in instances in which there previously had been none.

Interpretation (Bibring, 1954) strictly deals with unconscious material. It can refer to both defenses and that which is defended against. It often provides an explanation or a hypothesis about conscious behavior. Interpretations are often preceded by numerous clarifications. The following are examples.

Example 1: Clarification of Splitting

The patient described Pam as shallow, insensitive, and generally reprehensible.

Therapist: Wait a minute. Is that the same Pam that you described last week as one of the most wonderful people in the world?

Patient: Yes, that's her. What of it?

Therapist: I can't help but notice the rapid change in your thinking about her. Last week she was your best friend. Today she's despicable.

Example 2: Clarification of A Self-image

Patient: You know, doc, I'm just a little weakling. I don't exercise, I don't diet, I become short of breath when I walk a block. I don't know if I can survive. What if someone tried to rob me? I couldn't defend myself.

Therapist: You present yourself as little, helpless, and weak. What do you think about that self-image?

Example 3: Clarification of An Inferior-Superior Introjective Pair

Therapist: When you calmly state, as if it's a fact, that your wife is not curious about things and that she won't consider any change whatsoever, you convey the impression that you view her as an inferior person. At that moment you seem to view yourself as superior.

Example 4: Confrontation of Denial

Patient (after his seventh overdose): Doc, I feel great! This will never happen again. I can absolutely assure you of that!

Therapist: I don't want to be blunt, but you are using extreme denial. Just because you're feeling good at this moment, you insist that it will never happen again.

Example 5: Interpretation

Therapist: Could it be that your tendency to seek out such exciting and dangerous activities, in addition to your propensity to choose only the most exotic and sensual women, are both ways of avoiding and defending against those horrible feelings of emptiness and nothingness?

67. What Are the Supportive Interventions?

Supportive interventions include suggestion, therapeutic manipulation, abreaction, advice, reassurance, education, limit setting, reality testing, and provision of encouragement and praise. Unlike clarification, confrontation, and interpretation, these interventions, if used with any frequency, are more typical of supportive work.

Despite clear definition, interventions can and do overlap with each other. Some patients frequently "hear" one intervention when the therapist intends a different one. In some ways, suggestion is the polar opposite of interpretation. Yet, interpretations are sometimes understood and responded to as suggestions. I recall one example in which there were months of clarifications and interpretations regarding a patient's tendency to be attracted to troubled, needy, exotic women and to avoid more stable, professional ones. In therapy, this tendency was related to the patient's childhood fears plus fears of success, along with the recovering of early childhood memories regarding fears of attacks by the father. After months of interpretive work, the patient said: "So, what do I make of all this? What is the message that Dr. G is giving me? Ah, I've got it!! He wants me to stop going around with those women that I meet at the dances and to start dating Jewish doctors and lawyers."

68. What Determines the Therapist's Choice of Intervention?

Regarding the four large groupings, one can think of a continuum with normal-neurotic at one end and psychotic at the other end. The closer the patient comes to the normal-neurotic end of the continuum, the more the focus should be on insight-oriented techniques. Correspondingly, the closer the patient comes to the psychotic end of the continuum, the more the focus shifts to supportive interventions.

With patients near the middle of the continuum, the initial focus should be on insight-oriented techniques. Whenever these techniques prove to be insufficient, there is a change to more supportive interventions. In all cases, there should be a shift back to insight-oriented techniques whenever possible. With patients in the psychotic grouping, there is a preponderance of supportive interventions. However, even here one should shift to insight-oriented techniques whenever reasonable.

Regarding clarification versus interpretation, numerous clarifications are usually needed to prepare the way for interpretations. Thus, in the early phases of therapy, clarifications predominate. Interpretations play a larger role later. Interpretations are more common in therapies in which the patients are near the normal-neurotic end of the continuum.

69. Regarding Interventions, What Is a Good Approach at the Beginning of Therapy?

In initiating psychotherapy, the therapist should have as few preconceived ideas as possible, allowing the transference to unfold and selecting his or her interventions in accordance with this unfolding. The initial stance is one of exploration and clarification; deviations from this stance are in accordance with occurrences within the therapy hours.

If, by clarifications alone, the patient is reasonably comfortable, talkative, and motivated, no other interventions are needed. Whenever there is an obstacle to this positive position, attempts are made to resolve the obstacle. Insight-oriented techniques are tried first. If these techniques prove to be insufficient, more supportive techniques are used. Thus, if the patient is relatively talkative and has only a mild idealization of the therapist, the therapist might confine himself or herself to clarifications. If the patient refuses to leave the office after the session, the therapist might revert to suggestion and limit setting. If the patient seems very perplexed with the therapy, the therapist might add a bit of education. As noted, after a supportive intervention is initiated, the therapist should shift back to insight-oriented techniques whenever reasonable.

70. Are the Manner and Style of the Intervention Important?

The manner and style in which the intervention is delivered, in addition to the wording, are of obvious importance. An empathic attitude with a relatively "neutral" stance is always desirable. A confrontational, aggressive, or defensive stance is to be avoided. Before initiating any intervention, one should try to be as free of feelings as possible. It is common to offer an interpretation when one has been provoked, in the guise of helping the patient understand. The unconscious motive of the interpretation is retaliation. Although interventions made in this manner might well be accurate, they usually lead to arguments and battles, greatly detracting from the therapeutic alliance. Alternatively, supportive interventions are often offered prematurely when one either feels guilt or openly sympathizes with the patient. A good rule of thumb is not to offer any intervention when one is feeling strong affect. Simply wait and think!

In the following example, it has already been established that Jacob is Jewish. In the vignette, the therapist is also Jewish.

Patient (laughing): Jacob, the handyman, came over to the house the other day. You really have to be careful when he gets in the house. No matter what, he'll find something to fix. Wants to get me to pay him as much as possible. (*a little later*) Irv told me that after the [Jewish] service, he got together with a group of friends and talked about how they could make more money. And that seems to be their number one priority.

Therapist (feeling attacked himself): You seem to be very picky today. First you come in and don't bother to close the door. Then you spend 5 minutes criticizing the book you see on my desk, going out of your way to discover the title. Then you make several hostile comments about Jews. What are you so angry about anyway?

A better comment than this very defensive confrontation might have been the following: "A number of times in the past when you have expressed criticism of Jews, it turned out that you were angry at me. Do you think that could possibly be happening here now?"

The first response, made with an edge, invites more criticism and a battle between patient and therapist. The second offers an opportunity for more collaborative exploration.

In the next example, the patient appears soaking wet.

Patient (coughing and complaining): It was so difficult getting here. I left my umbrella at work, then had to walk two blocks to your office. And I'm just getting over a cold.

I just feel so bad! (*sobs a bit*) I wish I could have a cup of hot chocolate.

Therapist: I don't have any hot chocolate, but I can offer you a cup of coffee. And here, have a cough drop.

Although the therapist's response here does not seem unreasonable, it does not offer the patient a chance to explore any transferential feelings related to her feeling victimized. Had the therapist not responded so reflexively, the theme of blaming the therapist for the inconvenience might well have come up. This would have allowed the exploration of the victim role in the transference. Depending on a number of factors, being supportive might not be contraindicated. What was contraindicated was the therapist acting so rapidly and so much in accordance with his or her own feeling. If this practice had been engaged in repetitively, important themes would not have entered into the therapy.

71. What Is an Affirmative Interpretation?

Affirmative interpretations (Meissner, 1988; Schaffer, 1986) are made in such a way as to demonstrate an appreciation and an acceptance of what the patient is going through. They are experienced as empathic and respectful, and thus they are usually well received. Here the therapist might make a comment such as "It's understandable that you feel that way, given. . . . " Affirmative interpretations are particularly useful when one is dealing with patients in the narcissistic and borderline groupings.

72. What Are Preparatory Comments?

A strategy related to the affirmative interpretation is what I call preparatory comments. Here therapists, anticipating a negative reaction to their intervention, prepare the patient by comments made before the intervention. There are a wide variety of negative responses therapists might anticipate to their interventions. The patient might feel slighted or re-jected, insulted or criticized. In addition, he or she might feel misunder-stood or might become unreasonably angry or guilty.

In all cases, the anticipated negative reaction is based on responses to similar interventions in the past. The preparatory comments pave the way for the patient to be able to listen and respond to the intervention with a minimum of defensiveness. As with affirmative interpretations, preparatory comments are most useful with patients in the narcissistic and borderline groupings. As the treatment progresses, these preparatory comments become less necessary. Often the patient will let the therapist know when they are no longer needed. Examples follow.

Example 1

Therapist: I want to say a few words before my question. The last time I commented on a financial matter, you felt that I was showing off, dem-onstrating to you that I knew more than you about money. I want to assure you that I do not have that intent. With that in mind, I was won-dering about your reasoning when you refused to use an accountant for your taxes.

Example 2

Therapist: I have a feeling that you might object to this comment because it focuses on the transference. You've told me time after time that it's ridiculous to emphasize the transference, that you didn't come here to explore your relationship with me. Nevertheless, it might be useful to pick up on your earlier allusion that your dating the internist might have something to do with me.

Example 3

Therapist: I know you view yourself at times as unaccomplished and inad-equate, and I know that you hate it when I think of this as your view of yourself rather than reality. Nevertheless, when you say that you can't possibly take that job, I was wondering if that might have more to do with your sense of being a "loser" rather than with the actual difficulties involved in the work.

Example 4

Therapist: I want to say that I do not mean to be competitive with you. Actually, it's clear that you know more about internal medicine than I do.

Yet, I was wondering if your thinking that Bob should be placed on blood pressure medicine had more to do with your dislike of and anxiety about dietary restrictions for yourself than with Bob's minimally increased blood pressure.

Example 5: (late in therapy)

Therapist: I just want to say a few words. . . .

Patient (interrupting): I know, I know. You want to be certain that I don't interpret your comment as insulting. I've heard that one hundred times. Just get on with your comment. I get the point already.

73. Should Therapists Ask the Patient for Feedback on Their Interventions?

Borderline patients, in particular, have a tendency to distort the therapist's interventions, either with and especially without preparatory comments. In patients with this tendency, it is useful for the therapist to ask about the patient's understanding of an intervention. Patients are asked their thoughts and feelings about an intervention, and then the therapist comments on their remarks. With some patients, this process needs to take place on a regular basis. In asking for patient feedback, the therapist should start by being rather general. Depending on the patient's response, the therapist then can become more specific. Examples are as follows.

Example 1

In this example, the therapist's intervention is followed by a period of silence.

Therapist: What do you think about the comment I just made?

Patient: It seems reasonable enough to me. (*The patient then goes on to another topic.*)

Therapist: I notice that you're going onto another topic. Yet, I would like to return to my comment for a minute. I was wondering what feelings you had about what I said.

Patient: Well, to tell the truth, I thought it was a correct observation. But haven't we been over that before? It's not like you're telling me anything new. So what's the point?

In this example, the patient defended against his anger by avoiding any comment on the therapist's intervention. The therapist had to ask the patient to comment on the intervention twice before the patient finally responded with emotion.

Example 2

Therapist: What do you think about the comment I just made?

Patient: I think you are full of shit. I never think that way. To think that you think I'm that uncaring is very upsetting.

Therapist: I didn't mean that you were uncaring. It's already crystal clear that you are a very caring individual. I only meant that for a minute you seemed to focus on your own thoughts and lost track of what your student was saying. (*The therapist then goes on to elaborate on the specifics here.*)

Patient: Oh, I see what you mean. I guess you're right. I thought you were being very critical, but now I see that you're not. I didn't want to get angry at you, so I changed the topic. But I guess I really was angry.

Example 3

This situation occurs after the therapist asks the patient to comment on his intervention and the patient responds in a reasonable way.

Therapist: The last time I made a comment like that one, you had the idea that I was acting like a know-it-all, like your father.

Patient: That's true, and I felt that way again. But it was to a lesser degree. Actually I think I'm at the point where I can catch myself doing that, then not feel that way.

The first example did not include any distortion. The patient merely suppressed and avoided his anger by changing the topic. The second example involved a clear distortion of the therapist's intervention in which the patient felt severely criticized. The third example involved an appropriate response to the therapist's intervention. Here the therapist followed up because the patient had reacted severely to similar interventions in the past.

Some patients initially respond reasonably to an intervention and then, after the hour, distort some aspect of it and become upset. In instances in which this is a pattern, it is important, after the initial response, to point out the patient's tendency for delayed responses. For example, the therapist might say, "Your response to my comment seems reasonable. Yet I can't help but remember that the last time I made a similar comment, you told me that you couldn't sleep at all that night, and it was because of my comment. On that occasion you thought I was demeaning you, but you only had that idea after the session."

74. When Should the Therapist Answer Questions?

In classical psychoanalysis, questions are viewed as associations and, like any other thoughts, used primarily to enhance dynamic understanding. With this orientation in mind, questions are not answered unless there are clear reasons to do so. This stance is sometimes used not only in psychoanalysis, but also in psychotherapy. To make this approach reasonable, the patient is often given ample explanation for the technique prior to its use. For the "blank screen" model, with the therapist viewed as an outside observer, this stance might make sense.

When going from psychoanalysis to psychotherapy on the one hand, and from a classical to a more relational model on the other, this technique becomes questionable. It emphasizes the authority of the therapist and the inequality of the relationship, and provides a somewhat stilted ambiance. An alternative stance that I advocate for selected patients, controversial to some, is to answer questions unless there is reason not to do so. Having said that, a word of caution is needed. One needs to have clearly in mind what questions are "reasonable" to answer and what questions are not. When the therapist declines to answer, he or she might state reasons for doing so, then initiate a dialogue about these reasons.

75. How Does the Therapist Deal with Lateness?

Regarding lateness, minor characterological deviations need not be focused on early. With time, patients will usually bring up the lateness themselves, elaborating on such items as their desire to do one more thing, their tendency to not waste any time, their need to overschedule, and so forth. More significant lateness, however, can represent a major resistance requiring attention and intervention. Discussion of lateness should initially be from the standpoint of anxieties occurring in the therapy that lead to avoidance of the sessions.

76. How Does the Therapist Deal with Missed Appointments?

Missed appointments frequently relate to anxieties about the therapy. Depending on the patient and the phase of the therapy, I do one of two diametrically different things: I simply wait for the next session, or I call the patient. Regarding patients in the normal-neurotic grouping and patients (in all groupings) who have attended sessions regularly for a sustained period of time, the former is preferable. Usually, patients themselves will call and leave a message; if not, they are apt to bring up the missed appointment in the subsequent session. They will, it is hoped, try to relate their absence to factors within the therapy itself. If they do not make this connection, the therapist should. Care should be taken not to discount the alleged reasons for missing the appointment. Rather, one wonders whether "if, in addition to the reasons he or she has given, there could also be factors related to the therapy itself that played a role in the patient's absence."

With patients just beginning psychotherapy, with those who exhibit obvious and overt resistances to the therapy, and with those for whom I sense there could be a danger, I initiate a call. Often I offer to reschedule, sometimes without extra payment. The call and the rescheduling provide tangible evidence of my view that regularly scheduled sessions are mandatory if the therapy is to be effective. They also demonstrate obvious concern, which can be useful to certain patients. Regarding potential danger situations, only rarely have I initiated calls. In the case of a young woman with whom several suicide attempts had previously occurred without warning, my one and only call was of obvious merit. Forewarned that she was very upset about my upcoming vacation, I phoned her at her home during the scheduled therapy hour. She answered in a groggy state, having just swallowed a number of pills. Fortunately, she readily agreed to immediate hospitalization.

77. How Does the Therapist Deal with Gifts?

An old rule of thumb was that the therapist, when presented with a gift, would not accept it. Instead he or she would ask the patient to talk about the gift, in an effort to understand the motivation. Accepting the gift was considered "gratifying" the patient and undermining the task of understanding. This diction, of course, was mainly applicable to the insight-oriented therapies. Overlooked in this thinking was the hurt, injury, shame, and sometimes humiliation experienced by patients under these circumstances. Painful feelings related to rejection can occur even in the "healthiest" of patients and are sometimes minimized by the therapist.

A better rule of thumb is to politely accept the gift, noting whatever the patient says about it. Then when the opportunity avails itself, a discussion of the dynamics can be initiated. This discussion need not occur immediately; it can wait until it spontaneously appears in the therapy. Exceptions include gifts offered as bribes, and those clearly unrealistic financially. Both of these are rare. In my career I have never experienced the former, and only rarely the latter. Although multidetermined, many gifts are first and foremost expression of loving feelings and should be recognized as such.

78. Are Self-Disclosures Useful?

When using the "blank screen" model (for both psychoanalysis and analytically oriented psychotherapy), under the influence of neutrality, anonymity, and abstinence, intentional self-disclosures play little role. The avoidance of self-disclosures is still the preference of many of the classical tradition. When going toward a more relational model, with emphasis on the joint construction of the transference, intentional self-disclosures can play a larger role.

The adjective "intentional" is used, because in all therapies there are numerous unintentional and unconscious self-disclosures. The office setting, the appearance and dress of the therapist, the way the therapist relates to the patient (including affect, animation, choice of words, accent, style, and frequency of interventions), his or her manifest personality, his or her preferred theoretical model, the countertransference, plus many other factors, offer unending sources of information about the therapist. These sources of information can be considered unintentional self-disclosures. Additionally there are unconscious "slips" or acts by the therapist. It is the ubiquity of these unintentional and unconscious self-disclosures that leads some (Aron, 1996; Renik, 1996) to question why therapists are so cautious about self-disclosures.

Regarding intentional self-disclosures, there are many different types. Renik (1999), for example, routinely advocates a type of self-disclosure that involves the therapist revealing his or her thinking (sometimes in detail) about interventions he or she makes to the patient. Relational therapists frequently encourage a focus by the patient on the therapist's subjectivity, with selective self-disclosures as part of this process. Many therapies include disclosures of "quasi" personal information, including such items as the therapist's vacation plans, marital status, hobbies, plus political and other opinions he might hold. Psychotherapy sometimes includes some informal chitchat about mutual interests, such as restaurants, sports, or finances. On occasion, direct advice is given to selected patients.

The question remains about whether these intentional self-disclosures are useful. Regarding psychotherapy that emphasizes the transference, this question becomes whether self-disclosures inhibit or contribute to the intensification and resolution of the transference, with ultimate therapeutic gain. Those against self-disclosures believe that they inhibit and distort that process. Those in favor believe that selective self-disclosures help establish a comfortable and safe milieu, enhancing the patient's ability to speak easily and openly, ultimately enhancing the therapeutic process. Regarding more supportive psychotherapy, there is a general tendency toward a more liberal use of self-disclosures. Here the question becomes whether self-disclosures contribute to the ultimate therapeutic gain, without much concern regarding the transference.

Several final comments are in order. There is a danger when using self-disclosures of intruding into the therapy in a way that changes the focus from the patient to the therapist, in a manner that can detract from the primary task of therapy. Patients sometimes are too willing to partake in this distraction. Thus the neophyte therapist must be wary about the use of self-disclosures. A judicious employment of these, using less rather than more, makes sense. Later in one's career, after much experience and an enhanced understanding of the nuances and subtleties of this very complex subject, the therapist will be in a better position to formulate his or her own unique technique and strategy regarding self-disclosures.

79. What Is the 5-Minute Warning?

Some patients have difficulty leaving the session. The end of the session often feels like an abandonment or a rejection. The patient might say, "Don't you like being with me?" or "I know you can't wait to get rid of me so you can see your next patient." Various attempts to extend the hour, such as bringing up significant material near the end or waiting until the end to write the check, are common. One method of dealing with this difficulty in certain patients is the "5-minute warning." Here patients are simply told that there are 5 minutes left. This warning alerts them to speak of material they have excluded to that point. More importantly, it enables them to prepare themselves for the separation and to avoid a situation in which they feel abruptly cut off. Discussion of the desirability of this parameter needs to precede its initiation. Often it can be abandoned later in the treatment.

CHAPTER

Interventions Regarding
Anxiety and Defense

80. What Is an Intervention Regarding Anxiety and Defense?

Psychoanalytic "conflict" theory is out of vogue in a number of circles. Yet this theory can be very helpful to the beginning psychotherapist in dealing with his or her patients' anxieties, inhibitions, symptoms, and character traits. It frequently lends itself to easy therapeutic applicability.

Psychoanalytic theory relates neurotic anxiety to fears of bodily harm, fears of punishment, fears of loss of love (and rejection), and, sometimes, fears of loss of the object. This type of anxiety typically surfaces when one is pursuing a relationship with a member of the opposite sex (or a homosexual relationship), when one is trying to advance oneself competitively in the workplace, or when one is asserting oneself. Via classical theory, this relates to the upsurge of a drive (sexual or aggressive feeling), opposition by the superego to the drive, the creation of anxiety in the ego, a defense against the anxiety, and a symptom or an inhibition as a compromise formation. Of course, much of the preceding takes place unconsciously. Although the anxiety relates to a current situation, it has its origins in a situation of "danger" in childhood. One notes and points out the sequence of upsurge of drive, opposition by the superego, creation of anxiety, defense, and compromise formation, both within and without the transference. Often the drive can be linked to childhood dangers. Interventions of this nature, noting all or parts of the preceding sequence, are termed *interventions regarding anxiety and defense.*

Interventions regarding anxiety and defense are commonplace with patients in the normal-neurotic grouping. A framework involving this conceptual model is typically used with these patients for both psycho-analysis and psychotherapy. With some modifications, this framework can also be used with members of the other large groupings.

The ideas just described correspond to Freud's (1926) original theory regarding anxiety and defense. Brenner (1982) has extended this model by including depressive affect along with anxiety as a second affect state routinely defended against by the neurotic patient. According to Brenner, both anxiety and depressive affect are unpleasurable and initiate psychic conflict. The difference between the two is that anxiety is associated with an impending calamity, whereas depressive affect is associated with a ca-lamity that has already occurred.

81. How Does the Therapist Make Interventions Regarding Anxiety and Defense?

Interventions regarding anxiety (or depressive affect) and defense are made throughout the course of psychotherapy, in a variety of situations both within and without the transference. Interventions take the form of point-ing out the sequence of current precipitating event, upsurge of drive, op-position of the drive by the superego, creation of anxiety, defense against the anxiety, resulting compromise formation, and linkage of the drive to the childhood danger. These interventions need to be made piecemeal. Thus, at one time the focus is on what frustration triggers the upsurge of drive; at other times, the focus is on the opposition of the superego to the drive, on how the anxiety leads to the defense, on the relation of the current anxiety to the conflicts of childhood, and so forth. For the patient to gain lasting understanding and eventually make changes, these inter-ventions need to be repeated throughout the therapy. It is the repetitive nature of these interventions in a variety of settings that needs to be em-phasized. All of the components of the sequence do not necessarily have to be addressed to effect change; however, the more components addressed, the better.

The usual approach is to address the components of the sequence in the order that they appear in the therapy hours. Often the inhibition or symptom is addressed first, followed by the anxiety, the present-day feel-ings (the drive) that are defended against, the superego disapproval of these feelings, and, finally, the linkage to childhood conflicts. The compo-nents of the sequence need not necessarily follow in that order. The pre-ponderance of interventions within, as opposed to outside of, the trans-ference depends on whether the psychotherapy is primarily analytically oriented or primarily dynamically oriented.

82. What Are Everyday Examples of Interventions Regarding Anxiety and Defense?

A typical vignette involves a young man who is attracted to a young woman. An upsurge of sexual feeling in this young man is unconsciously related to his childhood attraction to his mother and his fears of retaliation by his father. His superego is mobilized and alerts his ego, whose response is to create anxiety. The anxiety triggers any one of a number of defenses, resulting in one of many possible symptoms (phobias, obsessions, dissociative states, etc.). Alternatively, the anxiety triggers an inhibition in the pursuit of the young woman, without overt symptoms.

The eventual goal of the therapy is to point out the sequence of the sexual feelings toward the young woman, disapproval of these feelings by the superego, the creation of anxiety, the defense against anxiety, the formation of a symptom or inhibition as a compromise formation, and the linkage of these current feelings to the unconscious feelings and fantasies of childhood. The pointing out of this sequence takes place piecemeal in accordance with the unfolding of the material in the therapy hour. Those aspects of the sequence that surface first are addressed first. The anxiety associated with pursuing the relationship with the young woman might be pointed out first. This might then be linked to the inhibition or symptom, then to the anxiety associated with the sexual feelings toward the young woman, then to the superego disapproval of the feelings, followed by a connection to unconscious childhood feelings and fantasies. All of the linkages might be made, or only some of them. As the patient begins to understand the linkages, he is in a position to alter his behavior.

In another common example, a young man is pursuing his PhD, competing for the No. 1 position in his class. He has passed all of his exams, has completed his research, and has only to put the finishing touches on his dissertation. At this point, he develops some kind of inhibition or symptom that prevents completion of the task. Here the success of completing the dissertation is unconsciously associated with the success of outdoing his father (winning the competition for the love of his mother), with the concomitant fear of retaliation by his father. The superego opposes this aggressive drive of childhood, and the ego signals anxiety in response. The anxiety triggers a defense that results in an inhibition or symptom as a compromise formation.

The goal in the therapy is to point out the linkages. The inhibition or symptom might be examined first, from the viewpoint that "something is stopping the patient from completing his dissertation." The anxiety can then be linked to aggressive strivings in relation to this task and to the patient's disapproval of these strivings. Finally, the linkage is made to unconscious childhood conflicts. Again the linkages are made piecemeal, in accordance with the unfolding of the material in the sessions. When the linkages are understood, the patient is in a position to overcome his inhibition.

83. Can Interventions Address Other Uncomfortable Affects and Defense?

In addition to anxiety and depressive affect, other uncomfortable affect states frequently occur. These include rage, embarrassment, shame, humiliation, uncomfortable grandiosity, and emptiness. These states occur most frequently in those individuals who are especially vulnerable to perceived slights, rejections, rebuffs, and disappointments. Such frustrations lead to the affect states just enumerated. More so than anxiety, these states can be excruciatingly painful and difficult to tolerate. Thus, they are defended against rapidly. The patient sometimes defends against these feelings through a variety of self-soothing and acting-out behaviors (for example, stimulating and dangerous acts, perverse sexuality, and alcohol and drug abuse).

In psychotherapy sessions, these affects can be dealt with similarly to anxiety or depressive affect. Interventions involving anxiety (or uncomfortable affect) and defense are often reasonable and useful. In the sessions, the dysphoric affect needs to be experienced and tolerated as much as possible. This tolerance must be followed by careful exploration of what frustrates the patient and how he or she typically responds to the frustration. The sequence of frustration, uncomfortable affect, and defensive acting out needs to be repetitively addressed. Linkage to superego opposition and sometimes to unconscious childhood conflicts can also be initiated. At times, this type of exploration can be augmented by an additional focus on the maladaptive consequences of the defensive behavior. When this is done, special care must be taken to maintain a neutral, nonjudgmental, and noncritical stance.

84. Can a Vignette Demonstrating Interventions Regarding Other Uncomfortable Affects and Defense Be Provided?

The case of Ms. G illustrates interventions regarding a number of uncomfortable affects, including overwhelming anxiety, emptiness, embarrassment, shame, and humiliation. In this vignette, there are continual disruptions in the therapeutic alliance; as a result, techniques addressing these disruptions are necessary before interventions regarding the uncomfortable affects and defense can be initiated.

Ms. G experienced difficulty with continuity, problems experiencing and identifying feelings, difficulty correlating the present and the past, and problems in understanding causal links. She was prone to periods of overwhelming anxiety and to psychosomatic symptoms to which she was unable to attribute any cause. At times, she experienced a blank feeling or a void. She engaged in a variety of stimulating and sometimes dangerous activities, including parachuting, rock climbing, and boat trips down dangerous rapids. On a number of occasions, there were accidents with severe injuries.

At the beginning of psychotherapy, Ms. G had no idea that there might be a linkage between her internal feelings and these dangerous activities. As might be imagined, the initial transference theme was an inability to experience any feelings toward the therapist. While there was a devaluation of the therapy in words, along with an expressed lack of understanding of how the treatment worked, there was evidence that the therapy played an increasingly vital role in Ms. G's life. Having difficulty with cause and effect, Ms. G began to attribute any feelings and occurrences in her life to the effects of the therapy. This was done in a global way and was certainly not in accordance with reality. Thus, if Ms. G had several good weeks, she would attribute that to the therapy. Likewise, she attributed psychosomatic symptoms and intense anxiety to the treatment. At these latter times, Ms. G experienced intense urges to terminate.

There was a necessary initial focus on alliance problems, because they continuously threatened the treatment. Whenever there was a reasonable modicum of therapeutic alliance, there was a focus on experiencing and identifying feelings and then correlating these feelings with precipitants. This took place mainly within the transference and was a very slow and tedious process. As the alliance was gradually strengthened, both by factors regarding the stability of the therapeutic environment and by a focus on disruptions in the alliance, there was more sustained work on the central issues. Ms. G gradually was able to link specific perceived slights, criticisms, and lack of interest by the therapist with dysphoric feelings. She experienced feelings of embarrassment, shame, and humiliation in response to these slights and criticisms but defended against them almost instantaneously. She likewise experienced a void, or a blank feeling, due to a perceived lack of interest by the therapist. As the work progressed, Ms. G was able to become more specific and less global in cause and effect regarding her feelings.

Only after several years of the type of work just described did Ms. G begin to learn to correlate her painful feeling states to defensive activities. Linkages between uncomfortable feelings and rapid defense were initiated only after linkages to precipitants (or frustrations) and feelings had been established. Of course, frustrations could be linked to feelings only after Ms. G was able to experience and identify her feelings. Thus, the initial focus was on experiencing and identifying feelings. This was followed by a focus on linking these feelings with precipitants. Finally, the feelings were linked to defensive acting out. As noted, this work could be accomplished only at times of a viable therapeutic alliance, taking place after much focus on alliance problems. By the end of a prematurely terminated treatment, Ms. G had some awareness of the correlation of her feelings (anxiety, embarrassment, shame, humiliation, rage, emptiness) to both her psychosomatic symptoms and her stimulating activities.

85. Can These Types of Interventions Be Made with Patients in the Psychotic Grouping?

Arlow and Brenner (1969) long ago proposed a model in which interventions regarding anxiety and defense were applied to psychotic patients. These authors maintained that the major differences between neurotic and psychotic patients were threefold. In psychotic patients, regressions tended to be more severe and more pronounced, conflicts over the aggressive drive were more frequent, and disturbances of ego and superego functioning were more severe. If these three differences could be taken into account, psychotherapeutic interventions with psychotic patients would be analogous to those with neurotic patients. Although others (Bak, 1970; Freeman, 1970) vehemently disagreed with these ideas, this model is certainly applicable to some psychotic patients.

86. What Differences Are There When Using These Interventions with More Troubled Patients?

There are a number of important differences when interventions regarding anxiety and defense are used with patients more troubled than the typical neurotic. Patients in the more troubled groupings sometimes experience anxiety in a manner similar to that of the neurotic. However, at other times anxiety is experienced as more severe and more difficult to tolerate. This problem is related both to the intensity and primitivity of the aggressive drive and to the harshness and severity of the superego that opposes the drive. In addition to anxiety (or depressive affect), other affect states occur that are exquisitely uncomfortable. These include rage, embarrassment, shame, humiliation, emptiness, and, sometimes, excitement and grandiosity. Defenses against these states can be more primitive and can include immature, borderline, and psychotic mechanisms. Sometimes these defenses are accompanied by alterations in reality testing. Taking into consideration differences in the intensity of the anxiety (or uncomfortable affect), the harshness of the superego, the repertory of defenses, and the reality basis of the anxiety, interventions analogous to the defense interpretations in neurotic patients can and should be made.

87. What Happens When the Affect Experienced in the Therapy Session Is Too Intense?

Interventions regarding anxiety (or uncomfortable affect) and defense, especially within the transference, can sometimes be associated with feelings that become very painful. In those instances, to avoid unreasonable disruptions, the therapist must monitor the amount of frustration in the therapy sessions. Hence, "titration" of the frustration in the therapy hours is sometimes necessary, in addition to exploration. On occasion, despite all efforts, acting out is of such magnitude that limit setting and structuring of the patient's life outside the therapy hours become necessary. This includes the use of day centers and even hospitalization. Temporary hospitalization at times of regression allows the therapy to continue with greatly reduced risks of disruptive behavior.

88. What Does the Therapist Do When the Patient Loses His or Her Observing Ego?

In therapeutic work involving anxiety (or uncomfortable affect) and defense, an observing ego is necessary. This observing ego enables the patient to stand back from the conflict, observe, and try to understand what is taking place. Sometimes a patient is able to comprehend the dynamics, yet at times of stress loses the ability to maintain the observing ego. Then the symptom or disruptive behavior occurs despite the understanding. In these instances, the therapeutic focus needs to be on maintaining the observing ego.

Mr. H, a high-powered, achievement-oriented professional, continually set exalted, idealistic, and often very unrealistic goals. He felt obligated to fulfil these goals at all times without exception. When he failed to meet his expectations, he criticized himself in a harsh and relentless way. He would verbally berate himself, at times for hours. These verbal "beatings" took the form of accusing himself of being undeserving, inadequate, a piece of trash. He shouldn't have been born; he deserved to die! "Beatings" took place in regard to a variety of events, ranging from not achieving more at work, to not being a better son or friend, and to seemingly insignificant occurrences such as not cleaning his room or failing to exercise. At times, Mr. H "beat" himself for having physical difficulties such as headaches or the flu.

In the course of therapy, Mr. H was able to attain a fair amount of insight. He understood the idealism and the grandiosity behind his unreasonable goals. He understood the extreme harshness and viciousness of his superego attacks. He understood the gratification involved in these attacks and how the attacks could be sexualized at times. He understood that the "beatings" stopped him from moving forward in work and with relationships. He understood the precipitants to the symptoms. He had a decent understanding of the genetic correlates of the problem, including specific early memories involving his parents and brothers. Although ameliorated somewhat in frequency and intensity, the "beatings" continued.

At this point, the therapeutic focus changed to an examination of how despite his understanding, the symptoms recurred. There was a direct focus on the observing ego. What stopped Mr. H from using his observing ego to take a look at what was happening, gain perspective, and take action to stop his symptoms? Exploration revealed that the failure to involve the observing ego was itself a passive defense against being assertive. The preceding type of exploration allowed Mr. H to eventually gain more control over his symptoms.

With Mr. H, the therapy, including the focus on the observing ego, remained at an exploratory level. Sometimes the work of invoking the use of the observing ego utilizes more suggestion. This more supportive approach is adopted if a more exploratory approach, such as that used with Mr. H, has been unsuccessful.

89. Are There Other Conceptual Models That Can Be Used Instead of Anxiety and Defense?

One does not need to use a therapeutic model emphasizing anxiety and defense. There are other reasonable frameworks that can readily be substituted. However, the model of anxiety (or uncomfortable affect) and defense, as elaborated in this book, is useful practically. In addition, it can easily be applied to patients in all four large groupings and to the entire continuum of psychotherapies elaborated in this book. For more information on alternative models, see Chapter 14 (Contemporary Schools of Thought).

12
CHAPTER

Special Issues and Problems

90. How Does the Therapist Deal with the Use of Primitive Defenses?

Primitive defenses include splitting, devaluation, primitive idealization, projection, projective identification, denial, omnipotence (Kernberg, 1975), and various forms of acting out and externalization. These are the defenses typically used by patients in the borderline grouping, especially at times of stress. When these defenses contribute to a negative transference or create a resistance to therapeutic work, rapid exploration is necessary. This is especially true regarding splitting, devaluation, denial, projection, and acting out. Idealization, omnipotence, and grandiosity also need attention, but the focus can often be delayed until there is a better therapeutic alliance. Mild forms of idealization can sometimes be used to help strengthen the alliance.

The use of primitive defenses is almost always maladaptive and destructive to the patient's life. Thus, one of the aims of psychotherapy is to point out these defenses and their negative consequences so that the patient can become aware of them and decrease their usage. Primitive defenses should be demonstrated, both inside and outside the transference, whenever reasonable. Interventions regarding primitive defenses can often be framed along the conceptual model of anxiety (or uncomfortable affect) and defense.

An example regarding splitting (as detailed previously in Chapter 10) follows. The patient described Pam as callous, insensitive, and generally reprehensible. She said that Pam was basically a horrible person and that people like her did not deserve to be alive.

Therapist: Wait a minute. Isn't that the same Pam you described last week as one of the most wonderful people in the world, the Pam you found so helpful when you were studying for your French final?

Patient: Yes, that's her. What of it?

Therapist: I can't help but notice the rapid change in your thinking about her. Last week she was your best friend. Today she's a despicable character.

This is an example of splitting outside of transference. After demonstrating the splitting mechanism, the therapist can begin to help the patient identify the events that precipitate the flips (from all good to all bad) in the splitting. The example continues:

Patient: I guess you're right. I hadn't really thought of it that way. It is kind of striking.

Therapist: I wonder how you came to see Pam so negatively?

Patient (thinking): Well, you know, I think I have an idea. I started to really detest Pam when she called at the last minute to cancel last weekend. She had a decent reason, but it didn't matter. I had looked forward to going out so much; then my weekend was ruined. How could she do that to me? I felt she didn't care about me at all.

Therapist: You were looking so forward to the weekend. Then when Pam canceled, it was so frustrating that you switched from viewing her as one of your best friends to hating her.

Patient: Now that you put it that way, you're right. I really did change my feelings.

After a number of examples of splitting, the therapist can generalize the patient's tendency to use the splitting defense, sometimes with its consequences. Later in the therapy with the patient in this example, the therapist makes the following statement: "You've now presented a number of examples where you flip-flop drastically in your feelings about people. The same person who was recently a great friend becomes an enemy. And always the flips to the negative are precipitated by feelings that you've been rejected, criticized, or slighted. Sometimes you act negatively toward those who have frustrated you and are later sorry. I remember you were quite upset when Pam wouldn't have anything to do with you for a month."

91. What Is Projective Identification, and How Is It Dealt with in Psychotherapy?

A common way of thinking about projective identification is as follows (Goldstein, 1991): A projection is followed by an interpersonal interaction in which the projector actively pressures the recipient to think, feel, and act in accordance with the projection. Coercive interpersonal interaction is the essential feature of projective identification.

According to the Kleinians, psychotherapy works by an unending series of projective identifications. The patient projects onto the therapist, interacts with the therapist in some way, and then reintrojects or reinternalizes the projected part after it has been processed and modified by the therapist. Because the reinternalized projection is an altered or modified version of the original projection, the patient changes accordingly. Thus, change takes place in psychotherapy through this process of projective identification without overt therapeutic intervention. The term *container* (Bion, 1967) has been used to refer to therapists who can tolerate and contain the projected feelings, including distress, chaos, hostility, neediness, and, for that matter, love.

In addition to the silent change that takes place via projective identification, the therapist can initiate active interventions (usually interpretive) demonstrating this mechanism. It is the interpersonal interaction component that is most conducive to initial intervention. Two examples of interventions regarding projective identification follow.

Example 1

Patient (walking into the office slowly with a dejected air): You know, doc, I'm just a little weakling. I don't exercise, I don't diet, I become short of breath when I walk a block. I don't know if I can survive. What if someone tried to rob me? I couldn't even defend myself.

Therapist: Again, you present yourself as little, helpless, and weak. What do you think that's about?

Patient (getting a bit annoyed): It's not a presentation, doc. That's the reality! You never believe me! But it's true. If someone tried to rob me, I'd just be defenseless. *(The patient escalates as he insists on the validity of what he is saying.)*

Therapist: You don't appear so little and weak when you argue with me and try to force me to agree with your image of yourself as pathetic.

Example 2

Ms. D, although she functioned in a highly competent fashion and was widely respected in her profession, frequently presented herself in therapy as inadequate, ineffective, and pathetic. She said she was a loser, was inferior to her colleagues, and was looked down upon and scorned by her fellow professionals. Ms. D insisted that her therapist view her in the same way that she saw herself and repetitively acted so as to get him to feel and to treat her that way. In a manner particularly annoying to the therapist, Ms. D acted as if it were a fact that the therapist agreed that she was little and inadequate. She elaborated one example after another based on the assumption that the therapist agreed with her. If the therapist made any comment indicating that he felt differently, Ms. D would argue with him and insist that he was being stupid and demeaning.

Therapist: I want to take a moment and point out what I think might be happening here. I have the feeling you might disagree with me, but I ask you to listen to what I say, then to view my ideas as one possibility. You have been presenting yourself as inferior and inadequate, a loser, as you call it. You have presented a number of reasons why you think this is so. Regarding this, there are two phenomena I want you to consider. The first is that you seem to be doing everything possible to get me to believe that negative view of yourself. You are arguing with me vigorously, and you seem to be trying to force me to feel that way. Secondly, you then act as if I have accepted that view of you, although I haven't said anything indicating that.

92. What are Enactments, and How Are They Dealt with in Psychotherapy?

Enactments are "symbolic interactions between therapists and patients which have unconscious meaning to both" (Chused, 1991). Usually an action by the patient is followed by a response from the therapist. Both action and response are primarily unconsciously determined. Although usually initiated by the patient, enactments can also be triggered by the therapist. Once considered the result of unwanted countertransference reactions, enactments today are generally considered inevitable and ubiquitous, constituting an integral part of psychotherapy.

When undetected, enactments can be problematic. When noted, explored, and understood, they clearly contribute to the psychotherapy process. The role of the therapist is to understand his or her contribution (as much as possible), then to help the patient to determine his or her own role. It is the understanding afforded by the enactment, and not the enactment itself, that enhances the psychotherapy process. Some enactments, however, provide a shared experience and an increased sense of collaboration that are themselves helpful. Additionally, the patient's sense of efficacy in being able to influence the therapist can play a constructive role.

The distinction between enactment and projective identification is sometimes made. Basically the concepts are similar, with subtle differences. The concept of projective identification does not demand a response by the therapist, whereas the concept of enactment does. This difference, of course, disappears if the therapist responds. Additionally, the term *projective identification* places more emphasis on the "coercive" interpersonal interaction. Whereas some see psychotherapy as an unending series of projective identifications, others view psychotherapy as an unending series of enactments.

93. How Does the Therapist Deal with Severe Acting Out?

Regarding the psychotherapy situation, acting out technically means to act as opposed to talk. In a more general sense, it is used to refer to overtly action-oriented behavior rather than symptoms or behavior traits. In a more specific sense, it refers to action-oriented behavior that is particularly self-defeating and self-destructive, such as suicide attempts, acts of physical aggression, and dangerous activities. Acting out in this latter specific way is the focus here. As a defense, acting out can be conceptualized dynamically in a manner similar to that of other defenses: as a compromise formation by the ego in response to drives, the superego, and external reality. Thus, interventions regarding acting out can be framed in accordance with the model of anxiety (or uncomfortable affect) and defense.

Regarding interventions, insight-oriented techniques are attempted first. Although these techniques are often successful with severe acting out, at other times they fail and need to be supplemented or supplanted by more supportive methods. Acting out is sometimes of such magnitude that, as noted earlier, limit setting and structuring of the patient's life outside the therapy hours become necessary. This includes the use of day centers and even hospitalization. Temporary hospitalization at times of regression allows the therapy to continue with greatly reduced risks of disruptive behavior. An example of severe acting out is provided subsequently.

94. How Does the Therapist Deal with the Suicidal Patient?

The first task in dealing with a suicidal patient is that of assessment. This is quite important, because one does not want to overemphasize recurrent suicidal ideation with little possibility of action; more important, one does not want to minimize suicidal ideation when the risk of acting is real. In addition to looking at the usual demographic data, one needs to pay close attention to the relevant dynamic factors.

Questions that need to be addressed follow. When and how frequently does the patient think of suicide? What are his or her suicidal fantasies? How does the patient typically deal with the fantasies? Does the patient think he or she might act on the fantasies? Under what circumstances?

Has there been any planning regarding action? Is there some urgency about acting? Has the patient had similar fantasies in the past? Has he or she ever acted? If so, how? If not, how did the patient prevent herself or himself from acting? What ideas does the patient have about what would happen if he or she acted? What are the patient's ideas about life after death? Does the patient have any ideas about joining those already deceased? Does the patient have any thoughts of revenge by killing herself or himself? What precipitates the suicidal fantasies? How has the patient dealt with the precipitants in the past?

Demographic and social data can be used to supplement the all important dynamic assessment. Factors that add to the risk of suicide (Kernberg, 1993) include the patient living alone, being single, being unemployed, having experienced a recent loss, having a history of an early parental loss, having a family history of suicide, having a severe physical illness, having experienced a recent failure, overusing alcohol or drugs, and being overtly psychotic.

If, after a thorough assessment, the therapist feels that there is an actual risk of acting out, either there has to be a plan that will prevent that or the patient needs to be hospitalized. Regarding the former, one possibility is someone being with the patient continually. At times, patients can be trusted to monitor their suicide potential themselves and to ask for hospitalization if necessary.

In cases of acute suicide risk with patients who are overtly depressed, overtly paranoid, or overtly psychotic, medication is often needed. Depending on the risk, the patient can be placed on medication either inside or outside the hospital. In cases of chronic recurrent suicidal ideation, there needs to be an arrangement between the patient and the therapist in which the patient agrees to a set course of action whenever suicide is seriously considered. Arrangements include calling the therapist, calling other designated individuals, going to the emergency room, being hospitalized, and so forth. A set order regarding these arrangements is sometimes spelled out. Thus, the patient might first call a designated individual. If this individual is unavailable, or if the talk ends without relief, the patient might call the therapist. If the therapist is unavailable, the patient will go to the emergency room. Of course, the patient always reports the details of all suicidal thinking in the subsequent therapy hour, during which the dynamics are investigated. Although arrangements such as these are not always effective in the early phases of treatment, they become increasingly useful as the therapy progresses, in relation to the strength of the therapeutic alliance and the patient's superego. Agreements should not be set up with drastic consequences, such as the termination of therapy, if they are not fulfilled. Rather, they should be initiated in the spirit that the patient will muster all conscious energy to adhere to them.

A vignette involving a teenage patient with severe suicidal ideation follows. This patient had been in psychotherapy for a number of years. Initially, she concealed her suicidal ideation. On several occasions, she came close to acting; fortunately, however, her "plans" were discovered by the therapist in time for "preventative" hospitalizations. As might be evident at this point, the establishment of a therapeutic alliance was quite difficult, with several brief terminations in the early years. Later, when the alliance became stronger, the patient was able to share her symptom of intermittent auditory hallucinations with the therapist.

With the sharing of the voices, the patient and the therapist were able to establish a sequence that the voices followed, which allowed for early hospitalization at times of clear suicidal threat, before there was legitimate risk of acting. The voices started as sounds and then progressed to inaudible words and, finally, to words that the patient could hear but that had no understandable meaning. The words then took on meaning, but the meaning was vague. Then there were vague suicide ideas, followed by clear suicide ideas and, finally, commands. In the command stage, the patient at first did not listen to the commands but then began to worry that she might. Of interest was the fact that the patient never thought the voices were those of other people; she always maintained reality in that she viewed the voices as her own.

As the patient was able to reveal the preceding sequence, it became rather obvious at what point hospitalization was needed. With the establishment of the sequence, patient and therapist felt comfortable working on the dynamics of the voices without fear of acting out. As the dynamics were elucidated in the therapy sessions, the sequence would stop, usually with the voices decreasing in the same order in which they had originally occurred. Precipitants to the voices were learned about first, followed by the vulnerabilities underlying the precipitants. As understanding increased, the voices decreased; by the termination of therapy, they had virtually ended.

In this vignette, the severe acting out could be contained only after a suitable therapeutic alliance had been established. At this point, therapist and patient were able to work collaboratively to use the sequence of voices as signals to impending acting out. As the voices came closer to signaling action, either dynamic understanding was successful enough to send the voices in the opposite direction, or hospitalization was mutually agreed upon. Before the emergence of a reasonable therapeutic alliance, only hospitalization could prevent action. In this vignette, the possibility of hospitalization and the establishment of a reasonable therapeutic alliance combined to make dynamically oriented therapy workable.

95. What Does the Therapist Do When Patients Show Problems in Reality Testing?

Some patients in the borderline grouping have a tendency toward reversible regressions in reality testing under stress. This is often demonstrated in the therapy hours by sudden periods of paranoid thinking. If the paranoid feelings are strong, rapid clarification of the reality situation is indicated. In contrast to more psychotic patients, borderline individuals easily accept these interventions. After the reality is clarified, dynamic understanding of the paranoid distortion can be initiated.

A patient was suspicious and quite bothered by the prospect that the therapist was recording the session with a tape recorder in his briefcase. When the therapist simply stated that this was not the case, adding that he would never tape the session without obtaining her permission, she accepted the comment and was totally satisfied.

Another example is provided by Ms. A, on her initial consultation. As she walked in the door, Ms. A stated, "Either you or Dr. B is a liar." She went on to explain that Dr. B had said that I had told him that I would be available for consultation the previous week, yet I told her that I had no time until now. She then demanded to know which one of us was lying. When I explained to her that I had told Dr. B that I had time on Tuesday the earlier week but that she had not called me until Wednesday, she seemed totally satisfied, calmed down, and related the reason for the consultation.

Regarding patients with more chronic delusions, a useful approach is to remain neutral about the delusional beliefs, listening attentively and asking for relevant clarifications. There is no need to comment on the validity of the delusions unless they enter the transference or unless the patient asks for the therapist's opinion. Often patients will not ask for the therapist's opinion for long periods of time. When they finally do ask, they are usually "ready" to hear ideas different from their own. At this time, the therapist first comments on her or his understanding of the patient's perspective, elaborating the reasons she or he feels that the patient has that perspective. The therapist might note that "it is understandable that the patient feels the way he does, given.... " The therapist then goes on to state that, despite the patient's perspective, he or she has a different view, and the therapist explains his or her alternative thinking. This type of intervention, when initiated with tact and respect, is usually well received. If the therapist is asked for an opinion early on, she or he uses the same type of intervention. The therapist might add that it would be useful to try to understand the differences between the patient's thinking and that of the therapist.

96. How Are Dreams Best Handled in Psychotherapy?

The use of dreams in psychotherapy varies greatly in accordance with both therapist and patient. Some therapists look for every opportunity to work with dreams; others deemphasize their use and importance. Likewise, some patients use dreams to enliven and deepen psychotherapy; others act as if they do not exist. Known as the "royal road to the unconscious" in regard to psychoanalysis, dreams usually play a more limited role in psychotherapy. Yet they can clearly enhance the treatment, leading to discussion of repressed ideas, childhood memories, and transference discoveries.

If the therapist wants to encourage the patient to discuss dreams, he or she needs to show an active interest whenever dreams are reported. When the patient first brings up a dream, it is useful to explain the technique of dream association, in addition to the concept of manifest versus latent content. The manifest content of the dream is the content as it is remembered. The latent content is the underlying meaning, discovered after the disguised portions have been understood. The technique of associating to dreams involves patients simply saying whatever pops into their mind regarding the dream. This is supplemented by their choosing selected portions of the dream and associating to those portions. In addition, the therapist might select elements of the dream and ask the patient for her or his thoughts. The associations to the dream help provide links from the manifest to the latent content.

After patients report their dream and associate, the therapist can help them to use the material in a number of different ways. These include demonstrating the state of the transference, illustrating dynamic issues in the here and now, uncovering new topics (often from childhood) for exploration, and searching for unconscious meaning. Depending on the state of the therapy and the patient, the therapist might emphasize the manifest content, the latent content, or the associations.

Some patients frequently describe their dreams, not so much to learn about themselves but to please the therapist. With these patients, the desire to please needs to be addressed, but not in a way that inhibits future reporting. Other patients use dreams as a resistance, finding it easier to discuss dreams than to discuss other conflictual material. Still others resist the interpretation of dreams by reporting the dream at the end of the hour without time to associate or by filling the entire session with descriptions of long, complex, convoluted dreams. When a dream is used as resistance, or when there is a resistance to associating to or discussing the dream, the therapist, of course, needs to point that out.

An awareness of the fundamentals of the dream process helps the therapist to understand and use dreams. Dreams are expressed in primary process, characterized by condensation, displacement, absence of negatives, absence of qualifiers, timelessness, mutually contradictory coexisting ideas, representation by allusion, and predicative identification. Whereas the waking person accepts identity only on the basis of identical subjects, the dreamer invokes predicative identification and accepts identity on the basis of identical predicates (Arieti, 1955). Thus, if two people are wearing identical shirts, they are assumed to be the same person, or if two people have like parts, they are assumed to be identical (*pars pro toto*). In a dream, there can be people from different times of life, one individual can take on characteristics of several different people, or one person can turn into another. One dream will reveal a highly logical manifest content, whereas another will seem totally incomprehensible.

Symbolism in dreams is unending. There are some "universal" symbols, in which specific manifest content typically represents specific latent content. When looking for the underlying meaning of the dream, however, it is better to follow the associations than to rely on these "universals." Another characteristic of dreams is that they invariably contain material from the day prior to the dream. This material is called the day residue. Looking for day residues is a way of linking the dream to the present.

97. What Are the Pros and Cons of Prescribing Medication?

The question here is not whether the patient needs medication. Rather, given that medication is indicated, is it best for psychotherapists to prescribe it themselves? Obviously, if one is not a psychiatrist, the dilemma is eliminated. If one can prescribe, there are pros and cons to doing so. Recommending or prescribing medications can be interpreted in different ways by the patient, including fantasies that the therapist has given up on psychotherapy, that the therapist views the patient as very "sick," or that the therapist wants to control or experiment with the patient. In contrast, a psychiatrist who does not prescribe might be viewed as withholding, sadistic, or ignorant. With the preceding in mind, it is important to explore in depth the patient's feeling about medication.

Once the psychiatrist prescribes, a shift can occur in which the medication becomes the main focus of therapy, with discussions about the medication taking up inordinate amounts of time. Battles can ensue between patient and therapist about the need and desirability of medication, the side effects, the dosage, or whether an alternative medication might be more useful. Some clinicians think that interactions surrounding the medication provide additional useful material aiding the understanding of the patient's conflicts. They recommend that the psychotherapists prescribe themselves, viewing that approach as a holistic one and noting that shifting the responsibility to another physician can create splitting. On the other hand, others feel that the addition of a psychopharmacologist can eliminate many issues that detract from the psychotherapy.

I have mixed feelings about this issue myself. With a number of patients, it seems reasonable to prescribe oneself, especially if the medication regime is uncomplicated. When dealing with difficult and demanding patients, especially when there are problems with finding the most appropriate medication, I often find it advantageous to have someone else medicate. I have had several experiences with psychopharmacologists that worked particularly well. One psychopharmacologist was able to drastically reduce a patient's medication with great benefit; I doubt that I would have attempted that. In contrast, another psychopharmacologist, in regard to a patient desiring less medication despite an obvious need to the contrary, insisted that the patient toe the line; I suspect I would have been more easily influenced by the patient.

The question arises regarding collaboration between psychotherapist and medicating psychiatrist. When one completes a psychopharmacology evaluation, it is appropriate to call the psychotherapist and discuss the recommendations at some length. After this contact, there is often little need to collaborate, except at times of emergency or to help with the psychotherapy. The latter is not really desirable; it sometimes occurs when the therapist has little experience or when the psychiatrist is overly controlling. Occasionally problems are created when therapists continually make suggestions about changing the medication, either to the patient or to the therapist. If the psychotherapist and collaborating psychiatrist have mutual respect for one another, the treatment usually progresses quite well, with minimum collaboration. Obviously there are exceptions.

13
CHAPTER

Phases, Trends, and Termination

98. Are There Phases or Trends in Psychotherapy?

Phases and trends in psychotherapy vary in accordance with the basic strategy. When the basic strategy is to maximize the transference, the early phase of treatment focuses on ways to enhance the development of the transference. As this is accomplished, a trend is for the patient's core conflicts to become progressively activated, worked through, and resolved within the context of the transference. Working through involves a process of repetition in which the conflicts enter the transference repeatedly and are correlated with both present-day problems and the childhood years. Psychotherapy assumes progressively greater importance to the patient as the transference intensifies and the patient works through her or his various issues. The therapy enters the termination phase after the conflicts have been sufficiently addressed and understood and the patient is in a good position to make constructive changes in his or her life. In the termination phase, issues of separation and loss are addressed. Obviously, the preceding outline is very schematic, varying greatly from individual to individual.

When the basic strategy is to maximize the therapeutic alliance and to use the positive alliance to help the patient understand his or her dynamics (by correlating the current conflicts with the past), the early phase of treatment emphasizes the establishment of a stable alliance. In those patients lacking in basic trust, this task can be very difficult, with the emphasis on strengthening the therapeutic alliance continuing throughout much of the therapy. A trend is to focus on the patient's core difficulties whenever the therapeutic alliance is sufficiently strong but to shift focus to repairing the alliance whenever there is a disruption. Related to this is a continual oscillation between focus on the therapeutic alliance and the core difficulties. As the alliance becomes strengthened, the trend is for more emphasis on the core difficulties and less on the alliance. Working through involves a repetitive focus on the core conflicts in a variety of settings, this time largely bypassing the transference. The termination phase begins when the conflicts are reasonably understood and the patient is in a position to make constructive changes in her or his life. Again, this phase addresses issues of separation and loss.

In patients with whom the basic strategy is to maximize the transference, but for whom there are also issues involving lack of trust, the focus is both on the establishment and maintenance of a positive therapeutic alliance and on the development of transference. Here the trends are similar to those just described (in which the strategy is to maximize the therapeutic alliance), except that interventions regarding core difficulties, initiated when the alliance is favorable, center on the transference.

99. When Does the Termination Phase Begin?

Ideally, the therapy enters the termination phase after patients' core conflicts have been sufficiently addressed and understood and they are in good positions to make (or continue to make) constructive changes in their lives. At this point, patients should have internalized the lessons of psychotherapy so that they can deal with life effectively without the help of the therapist. There is much individual variation in terms of how well patients have addressed and understood their conflicts and how well they have internalized their gains.

The subject of termination often comes up gradually, with the patient fantasizing about leaving long before seriously considering that option. When there is serious consideration, the therapist should address the topic, thoroughly exploring both the pros and the cons. If the patient is running from conflicts or from an uncomfortable transference, the therapist needs to address that directly. The approach of examining resistances to continuing the therapy is useful here.

Some patients, as soon as they feel reasonably well, think that they should terminate. These individuals view themselves as unworthy of treatment unless it is essential. For these patients, the focus needs to be on their low esteem and their self-defeating tendencies. I sometimes offer the suggestion that, rather than thinking of stopping as soon as the need is no longer overwhelming, an alternative perspective might be to think of continuing if the therapy is playing a positive role in the patient's life. In contrast to those individuals who wish to leave prematurely, some patients desire to remain in treatment indefinitely. With this group, the therapist needs to be active in addressing those fears that prevent the patient from considering termination.

When both patient and therapist feel that actual termination is reasonable, a date needs to be set. It is useful to set the date a number of months in advance to allow ample opportunity for examination of "termination issues." The length of the termination phase is dictated by the length of the psychotherapy, with longer therapies benefitting from longer terminations.

100. What Does the Termination Phase Involve?

The primary focus in the termination phase is on separation and loss. In addition, this phase can provide an opportunity for a review and a reexamination of some of the important themes of the psychotherapy. This is a calm and tranquil phase for a number of patients. For others, it can be an exceptionally difficult time, demanding focus on issues that are exquisitely sensitive for the patient. Especially with patients in the borderline and psychotic groupings, regression and acting out are to be expected.

Whenever possible, it is best to maintain regularly scheduled appointments, using the time to work through termination issues. For some patients, this might not be reasonable. Flexibility at this stage, with regard to scheduling, dealing with regressed and acting-out behavior, and changes in termination plans, is important. Some patients find the termination issues too painful to deal with and avoid them at all costs. Thus, there can be blanket denial or flights into health. Precipitous premature terminations to avoid uncomfortable feelings sometimes occur. Finding it easier to leave a negative situation than to deal with the pain of loss, some patients try to precipitate fights with the therapist or attempt to fault and devalue the therapist or therapy.

It is useful to set the termination date a number of months in advance. If the date approaches and the patient does not seem "ready" to terminate, the date can be pushed forward. With some patients, tapering the frequency of the sessions can make the process more tolerable, helping to decrease regression and acting out. For a few very fragile patients, it is best not to set a formal termination date. Instead, regular appointments, sometimes with increasing time intervals between sessions, can be scheduled indefinitely.

As termination approaches, it is useful for the therapist to tell the patient that he or she will be available on occasions of need, time and circumstances permitting. The patient is left with an invitation to both consult the therapist at times of stress and come back for a further course of psychotherapy should the desire arise.

Contemporary Schools of Thought

101. What Is Modern Conflict Theory?

Modern conflict theory, most clearly elaborated in Chapter 11, is the predominant theory of this primer. A contemporary version of classical psychoanalytic thinking, it focuses on dynamic understanding, emphasizing structural theory (the ego, the superego, and the id), and places special emphasis on the relation of anxiety and defense. Originating with Freud, but having many subsequent contributors, the theory was extended and most clearly presented by Brenner in 1982. The fact that Brenner (1994) more recently has revised a number of his ideas does not detract from the current significance and influence of his earlier writings. Today the terms *modern conflict theory, ego psychology, classical theory,* and *drive theory* are used interchangeably. I dislike the term drive theory, because it tilts analytic theory away from its current emphasis on the ego (and superego). Modern conflict theory does focus on biological and maturational factors, with emphasis on the unfolding of instinctual drives. Although downplayed in comparison with relational theories, interpersonal relations (what actually transpires between caretakers and the child), object relations (the internalized version of interpersonal relations), and child development, all play important roles in conceptual thinking.

The specifics of *anxiety and defense theory* are detailed in Chapter 11. With that in mind, only a brief summary will be presented here. Modern conflict theory relates anxiety to fears of bodily harm, fears of punishment, fears of rejection (and loss of love), or fears of loss of the object. Anxiety surfaces when one is pursuing a significant relationship, when one is trying to advance oneself competitively in the work place, or when one is asserting oneself in any situation. Theoretically, there is an upsurge of a drive (sexual or aggressive feelings), opposition by the superego to the drive, the creation of anxiety in the ego, a defense against the anxiety, and a symptom, inhibition, or character trait as a compromise formation. Although the anxiety is triggered by a current situation, it has its origins in a situation of "danger" in childhood. This process takes place mostly on an unconscious level. Brenner (1982) extended classical theory by including depressive affect (in addition to anxiety) as a second state routinely triggering defense. Additionally other (more painful) affect states—including rage, embarrassment, shame, humiliation, emptiness, and nothingness—can and should be included. With these extensions, I sometimes use the terminology *uncomfortable affect and defense* as opposed to anxiety and defense.

In the psychotherapy setting, to help elicit understanding, the therapist notes and points out the sequence of current precipitating event, upsurge of drive, opposition by the superego, creation of anxiety, defense, resulting compromise formation, and linkage to childhood events and dangers, both within and outside the transference. Interventions here are made in a piecemeal fashion. For the patient to gain lasting understanding and eventually make changes, these interventions need to be repeated throughout the therapy.

102. What Is Close Process Attention?

Within contemporary ego psychology there is now some controversy about two therapeutic approaches (Pray, 1996). The work of Arlow and Brenner (Arlow, 1985; Arlow & Brenner, 1964, 1990; Brenner, 1982) emphasizing compromise formation is contrasted with that of Gray (1994) and Busch (1999) emphasizing what has become known as *Close Process Attention*. Leaving out the reasons for this controversy, and without spelling out the details of the two approaches, I will touch on the basic differences.

Using their total experience regarding what they have learned about the patient from the therapy, Arlow and Brenner focus on inferences to unconscious conflict in the clinical data, as they relate to compromise formations. They point out those aspects of the id, ego, and superego that are unconscious at the time and that contribute to the compromise formation. The idea is "destabilizing the equilibrium of forces in conflict within the patient's mind" (Arlow, 1985) for the purpose of healthier restabilization. Gray and Busch, in contrast, demonstrate emerging drive derivatives and defensive shifts that occur in the here and now of the therapy hours. By paying close attention to the patient's flow of associations, and staying close to the surface, they demonstrate conflict as it occurs. Both Gray and Busch do this in a rather systematized way, in a manner that pays close attention to the patient's observing ego and to his sensitivities and vulnerabilities. They feel that this method diminishes the role of the analyst as an authority and enables the patient to gradually expand his or her conscious ego.

From the perspective of the sequence of upsurge of drive, opposition by the superego, creation of anxiety, defense, and compromise formation, Arlow and Brenner intervene to demonstrate any aspect of the sequence that shows the compromise formation, focusing on what is currently unconscious. Gray and Busch intervene to demonstrate defenses currently in operation in the hour. They then expand to other parts of the sequence. Arlow and Brenner's method is to make the unconscious conscious, whereas Gray and Busch use the patient's conscious ego to demonstrate conflict, starting with defense, as it appears in the hour.

As noted in the previous question, Brenner (1994) has renounced the structural model; that is, he no longer feels it helpful to use the structural terminology. Yet psychotherapeutically, his technique remains unchanged. He now speaks in terms of *drive derivatives, opposition to these derivatives,* and *defense,* without reference to the terms *ego, id,* or *superego.*

103. What Is the Relational School?

The relational school of psychoanalysis, together with self psychology and object relations theory, present the main contemporary challenges to ego psychology. Spearheaded by Greenberg and Mitchell (1983), the relational school originated in the 1980s as a reaction to classical drive theory. At that time, Greenberg and Mitchell proposed two mutually exclusive models of the mind—the *drive-structure* and the *relational-structure* models. Initially, these authors insisted that these two models, one emphasizing the biological unfolding and discharge of the drives, and the other emphasizing the role of actual early relationships, were incompatible. In its exuberance to challenge the prevailing predominant ego psychology, relational theory was quite inclusive, offering a place for many contrasting theories, all rebelling against the "drive" model. Although contemporary, the origins of relational theory go back to Ferenczi (1932), who is credited with initiating the first important shift from Freud's method. Today there is overlap between relational theory, intersubjectivity, and social constructionism. Intersubjectivity, although more associated with self psychology, can be quite similar to the relational school, whereas social constructionism has been virtually incorporated in the relational world.

Included within relational theory are various self psychological, object relational, and interpersonal modalities. Relational theory can be seen as a contemporary eclectic theory, emphasizing the centrality of the relationship (Aron, 1996).

The emphasis of the relational school is on the dyadic, the interactive, the interpersonal, and the intersubjective. The psychotherapeutic experience is an intersubjective one, in which the transference is thought to be jointly created by patient and therapist. Emphasis is on coparticipation, mutuality, new experience, and authenticity. These are sometimes contrasted with anonymity, abstinence, neutrality, and the repetition of old experience. Although mutuality is emphasized, the psychotherapy experience is thought to be asymmetrical, in that therapist and patient participate in different and unequal ways. Teicholz (1999) posits authenticity or authentic engagement as the primary mode of intervention by the relationalists, contrasting that with interpretation by the ego psychologists, and empathy by the self psychologists.

Focus is on the establishment of a safe environment, in which the patient can participate with few constraints and great freedom, reenacting his early relational patterns within a new relationship. Here the therapist enters the patient's relational world and fully and freely engages in transference/countertransference enactments. Relational theory claims to maintain a balance between perspectives: internal versus external, intrapsychic versus interpersonal, subjective versus intersubjective, and one person versus two persons.

104. What Is Self Psychology?

Self psychology began when Kohut (1971, 1977, 1984), working and dealing within the framework of classical psychoanalysis, described the spontaneous emergence of one of several elaborately described transferences (the mirror, the idealizing, and the twinship) during the course of analysis. Initially focusing on the narcissistic personality, self psychology has expanded into a general theory of psychoanalysis and psychotherapy, currently rivaling ego psychology, the relational school, and object relations theory for popularity and influence.

Most important to self psychology is the emphasis on empathic immersion (or vicarious introspection). Initially described by Kohut as an aid to eliciting material and obtaining understanding, empathy has come to be viewed as a process that itself can promote psychic development and structure. Also central to self psychology is the focus on the self in relation to *selfobjects*. Selfobjects are viewed as people who provide functions necessary to maintain a dependent individual's psychological integrity. Although selfobjects are initially experienced as part of the self by the individual, the degree of separation of the self from the selfobjects decreases later in life. Emphasis is on the importance of self/selfobject relationships from birth to death. Although the quality of the self/selfobject relationship changes from primitive to mature, the importance of these relationships for needed self-cohesion and self-esteem remains relatively constant. Self/ selfobject relationships additionally provide enhancing experiences such as soothing comforting, strengthening, validation, and vitality. Selfobject needs are ubiquitous, occurring in all relationships. In the therapeutic situation they appear as selfobject transferences. These selfobject transferences are thought to operate overtly on the foreground or silently in the background.

Kohut initially believed that primitive selfobject transferences were either eliminated or converted to more mature selfobject transferences by the process of transmuting internalization under optimal frustration. More recently, Bacal (1998) has adopted the concept of optimal responsiveness to replace that of optimal frustration. Thus a contemporary self psychological perspective focuses on the conversion to mature selfobject transferences under optimal responsiveness. Other current emphases of self psychology include a focus on affects, especially those of shame, embarrassment, humiliation, and rage, as well as the concept that destructive aggression and/or pathological sexuality are byproducts of an oedipal phase gone awry.

Just as modern ego psychology has advanced beyond Freud, so has self psychology moved beyond Kohut. This is evidenced by converging and diverging themes in contemporary self psychology, including the work of Goldberg (1988, 1990), Stolorow, Brandschaft, and Atwood (1987), Lichtenberg (1989), Lichtenberg, Lachmann, and Fosshage (1989, 1992, 1996), Wolf (1988), Bacal (1998), and Shane, Shane, and Gales (1997). Some talk of the self psychologies instead of self psychology. There are at least four contemporary groupings in self psychology. The "classical" self psychologists (Wolf, 1988) stay close to Kohut, while modifying and modernizing a number of his ideas and concepts. The intersubjectivists (Stolorow, Brandschaft, & Atwood, 1987) emphasize the intersubjective (two person) aspects of all interactions, from birth onward. Although originating outside of self psychology, and similar in a number of ways to the relational perspective, intersubjectivity is considered within the domain of self psychology. The motivational systems approach of Lichtenberg (Lichtenberg, 1989; Lichtenberg, Lachmann, & Fosshage, 1992; 1996) emphasizes five motivational systems within the context of contemporary infant research and a self psychological intersubjective framework. The five motivational systems—regulation of physiological requirements, attachment/affiliation, exploration/assertion, aversion, and sensual/

sexual—can be contrasted to the dual drive theory of classical psycho-analysis. Finally, the work of Shane, Shane, and Gales (1997) emphasizes attachment and systems theory within a self psychological context that borrows heavily from the relational perspective.

105. What Is Intersubjectivity?

Intersubjectivity (Natterson & Friedman, 1995) refers to the mutual influence of the subjectivities of two people in a relationship. This influence includes both conscious and unconscious aspects. In therapy, the relationship, of course, is between the therapist and patient. Emphasis is on the continual, mutual, reciprocal, and interactional influence of each person on the other.

Intersubjectivity was popularized by Stolorow and Atwood (Atwood & Stolorow, 1984; Stolorow, Brandschaft, & Atwood, 1987), who linked their perspective with self psychology. Given this association, intersubjectivity is currently thought to be one of the movements within self psychology. Although this movement adheres to the main themes of self psychology, it differs in its emphasis on the discovery of (unconscious) organizing principles as opposed to the elucidation of selfobject relationships. Intersubjectivity has also been adopted by the relational school. The intersubjective approach of this school is similar to that of Stolorow and Atwood, except that it is incorporated in a relational instead of a self psychological model.

There is an important difference between the intersubjectivity of Stolorow and Atwood and that of the relational movement. Stolorow and Atwood speak of intersubjectivity whenever two people are together, unrelated to their developmental levels. Many of the relationalists (Benjamin, 1990; Stern, 1985) view true subjectivity more as a developmental landmark. Benjamin (1988), for example, does not speak of subjectivity until the child is able to conceptualize the other (the mother) as a person with her own needs and desires, separate from the child. Thus Benjamin differentiates the mother as an "object," whose sole purpose is to meet the child's needs, from the mother as a "subject" with her own distinct needs and desires.

With the focus on the mutual and reciprocal relationship between patient and therapist, the unfolding of the psychotherapy and the transference is thought to be jointly determined. Equality between patient and therapist is emphasized, and authority downplayed. The therapist is thought to be implicitly revealing of himself by definition. However, deliberate self-disclosures need not be part of the intersubjective approach.

106. What is Social Constructionism?

There is a large overlap between social constructionism, the relational school, and intersubjectivity. Social constructionism, in fact, is usually considered a movement within the relational school. The term, originally proposed by Hoffman (1983), emphasizes the joint construction of the transference and psychotherapy process by patient and therapist. "Social" refers to the therapy as a social interactive process (Natterson & Friedman, 1995).

Psychotherapy is thought to unfold in accordance with the subjective and unconscious experiences of both therapist and patient. With this in mind, the effects of the therapist's interventions cannot be known in advance. Thus the psychotherapy process is uncertain and ambiguous. The authority of the therapist is diminished, and the therapist is "freed" to be more open, more spontaneous, and more authentic. The process is seen to be interactive, mutual, and bidirectional.

All of the above are relative. Thus Hoffman (1996) views the psychotherapeutic process in terms of dialectics. There is the dialectic between the therapist as an authority and the therapist as a person like the patient. Additionally there is the dialectic between the repetition of old experience and the construction of new experience. Therapeutic action, as in more classical therapy, results from understanding based on the transference, but the transference is viewed in a different, more interactional, coconstructed way.

107. What Is Object Relations Theory?

Object relations theory is a term that can be applied to a number of psychoanalytic theories. In the usual (narrow) sense of the term, it refers to the British object relations school—Melanie Klein (Segal, 1981), Fairbairn (1954), and Winnicott (1958), and their followers, including Guntrip (1961) and Balint (1968). More modern revisionists of object relations theory include Edith Jacobson (1964) and Otto Kernberg (1976), both of whom combine object relations theory with ego psychology. Some view the work of Margaret Mahler (Mahler, Pine, & Bergman, 1975) as part of the object relations school. Additionally there is an American object relations group, including Hamilton (1988), Althea Horner (1991), and others. This school, in some ways, appears "close" to ego psychology. Finally, the work of Kohut (1971, 1977, 1984) and the self psychologists is considered by some to be within the realm of object relations.

Object relations theory involves the focus on early interpersonal relations and their internalization. The main emphasis is on the outcome of the internalization process, as represented by internal objects, introjects, self and object representations, and other forms of internal structures. With the above in mind, object relations can be differentiated from interpersonal relations in the following way. Interpersonal relations are personal interactions that actually take place between individuals, either in the present or the past. Object relations are the internalized derivatives of these interactions. Although the different schools of object relations vary considerably, they all center on internal structure (introjects, self and object representations, etc.).

In the broadest usage of the term, object relations theory can apply to all psychoanalytic schools, as all incorporate object relations within their thinking. The relational school would certainly welcome the object relations theorists within their group; alternatively, the relational school could be thought of as part of the object relations group. As noted, self psychology and intersubjectivity are included by some in the object relations camp. Ego psychology also incorporates object relations; there object relations are considered as one of several important ego functions.

108. Is It Advantageous to Mix and Integrate Different Models?

There are clear differences of opinion regarding the desirability of integrating different models. One opinion is that it is best to adopt one model, become thoroughly familiar with it, and apply it systematically and consistently. Some feel that the application of one model in this way, even if it is not the "preferred" model, provides a better framework than mixing different approaches. An alternative, of course, is to borrow from several different models, flexibly mixing and matching, in an effort to best meet the needs of each individual patient. My own feeling is that it is desirable to initially become thoroughly grounded in one particular school of thought, but that once that school is "internally" established, there is much room for integrating other models.

I integrate in two different ways. First, I use one theory as my base, but incorporate aspects of several others into my usual framework in a daily and regular way. To be more specific, I emphasize modem conflict theory but draw consistently from selected aspects of self psychology and the relational school. By focusing on self and object representations, I also incorporate object relations theory. This "integrated" approach is consistent with all my patients. Second, when dealing with particular patients, I sometimes additionally modify my technique by combining models in different ways.

109. How Do Therapists of Different Models View Each Other?

In this era of multiple models there is a tendency toward more openness within the various competing frameworks. Yet there still is too much polarization between the various schools, with too much idealization of one's favorite model. It is sometimes amazing how much inflexibility therapists show when it comes to giving reasonable consideration to alternative thinking. This inflexibility often seems related to the personality style of the individual. I often wonder how an adamant Freudian, for example, would see things if he had been "brought up" on a Kohutian framework. Probably he'd be an adamant self psychologist.

APPENDIX
A Look at the Ego Functions

A-1. What Is the Purpose of a Focus on Ego Functions?

An effective way of both describing and understanding patients is through the study of ego functions (Goldstein, 1985). This approach aids in achieving diagnostic clarity and conceptual understanding, in therapeutic assessment, and in determining prognosis. It can be thought of as a bridge between descriptive and dynamic psychiatry, in that the ego functions can be examined descriptively or can be viewed as an aid to dynamic understanding.

Freud's structural model (1923) differentiates the id, the ego, and the superego. According to this theory, the ego emerges from the id in a gradual and ongoing process, one that is well consolidated by age 3. Once formed, the ego becomes the chief mediator between the individual and the external world. It is the executive agency of the mind, continually interrelating, influencing, and being influenced by the instinctual drives, the superego (once that structure is formed), and the external world. All action takes place through the ego.

Freud (1940) later described the ego as having a number of principal characteristics. Anna Freud (1936) and Hartmann (1939) were among the first to list and describe various functions of the ego. More recently, Beres (1956) and Bellak (1958) conceptualized seven ego functions:

1. Relation to reality
   a. Adaptation to reality
   b. Reality testing
   c. Sense of reality
2. Regulation and control of drives
3. Object relations
4. Thought processes
5. Defensive functions
6. Autonomous functions
7. Synthetic-integrative function

Bellak (1970) and Bellak and Meyers (1975) added several other ego functions: judgment, adaptive regression in the service of the ego, stimulus barrier, and mastery-competence.

Regardless of the classification of ego functions employed, one can take an "ego inventory" and focus on specific ego strengths and specific ego weaknesses of the patient. This "ego inventory" can be thought of as a detailed description of the individual. It is sufficient to establish a differential diagnosis among the four major groupings of psychopathology: the neurotic, the narcissistic, the borderline, and the psychotic. We will now examine several of the ego functions.

A-2. How Does One Conceptualize Reality Testing?

Reality testing, together with the sense of reality, and the adaptation to reality, are the trio of ego functions relating to reality. Reality testing is the ego function most assessed when considering the diagnosis of psychosis. In fact, psychosis has often been defined as a defect in reality testing. There are at least two ways of conceptualizing disturbances in reality testing. The first way, more commonly used, expresses global defects; it defines impaired reality testing as the inability to distinguish internal from external stimuli, or as the inability to tell what is occurring within one's mind from what is occurring in the outer world. This dysfunction in reality testing can be related to the concept of defective ego boundaries, as described by Federn (1952). Ego boundaries, in Federn's concept, are actually better understood as "self" boundaries. The inability to differentiate self representations (or images) from object relationships (or images) is intimately related to this definition of defective reality testing. Delusions and hallucinations are the best examples of defects in this aspect of reality testing.

The second way of describing impaired reality testing, much more subtle and common, is related to the distortion of present-day reality by infantile fantasies and infantile self and object representations. This type of defect to some extent is universal. Psychotherapy is helpful in lessening this kind of "distortion," yet it is almost impossible to eliminate entirely. An example is provided by a 33-year-old woman who, whenever confronted with a neutral or ambiguous message from a friend or acquaintance, interpreted the message to mean that the person did not like her. An infantile self representation of herself as bad and unlikable caused her to feel others also viewed her this way. This distortion occurred only when there was some ambiguity or stress.

This second kind of reality distortion is somewhat benign and occurs in neurotic as well as more troubled individuals. It is the first kind of reality impairment, the inability to distinguish internal from external stimuli, that is more specific to psychotic and borderline individuals. The psychotic shows major impairment in this area, either constantly demonstrating distortions in reality testing or continually using energy to prevent these reality distortions from surfacing. The borderline patient, in contrast, has a vulnerability, rather than a major impairment, in this area. In day-to-day functioning, the borderline patient maintains reality testing without a constant expenditure of energy, but remains vulnerable and sensitive to reversible regressions in reality testing under stress.

A-3. What Is Sense of Reality?

An intact sense of reality is shown by the ability to experience one's self and body, along with external events, as real and familiar. This ability differs from reality testing in the emphasis on experience and feeling. Confused body images, feelings of estrangement, derealization, depersonalization, and deja vu phenomena are common examples of defects in the sense of reality.

It is common for individuals to experience difficulty with the sense of reality while maintaining reality testing. Unlike reality testing, periodic disturbances in the sense of reality are not confined to more disturbed people; they can occur in many neurotic and so-called normal individuals.

A-4. What Is Adaptation to Reality?

Adaptation to reality is basically a measure of how one copes with and relates to the external world. There are some individuals who adapt effectively despite obvious impairments in other ego functions, such as reality testing. Thus, adaptation to reality is an important function to examine in patients who struggle with impairments in reality testing.

The story is told of a psychiatrist who saw an individual whom he had previously treated for a considerable time. The patient was walking across the street in the business district of a large city. The psychiatrist approached the ex-patient and politely asked how he was doing. The patient replied that he felt fine, that he was doing well, and that he was now a stockbroker earning $220,000 a year. After departing, the psychiatrist decided that he really wanted to ask his ex-patient one more question. So he ran to catch up with him and inquired, "Do you remember seven years ago, when you felt that there was an influencing machine in your late grandmother's attic, with gamma rays extending from the machine to your arms, legs, and genitals, then extending back to the planet Uranus?"

The patient calmly replied, "Yes." The psychiatrist continued: "And do you remember that you were certain that this machine was exerting control over you and your body, influencing you to do what your late grandmother wanted you to do?" Again the patient calmly replied, "Yes." The psychiatrist then asked the final question: "Whatever happened to that machine?" The patient replied, "Nothing. It's still there, and it's still working. Yet it no longer makes me anxious, and I don't tell anyone about it anymore." The moral of the story is that some people can have rather pronounced delusions or hallucinations in selected areas and still adapt adequately to reality. Isolated delusions and hallucinations of this type, that do not greatly impair adaptation to reality, are most commonly found in chronic schizophrenic patients.

A-5. How Does One Think About Impulse Control and Frustration Tolerance?

Impulse control is the ability to cope with impulses or anxiety without acting. "Acting" here includes direct discharge, symptom formation, or regressive behavior. Frustration tolerance is a measure of how much additional frustration or anxiety an individual can tolerate before acting. Poor impulse control and poor frustration tolerance are concomitant, and in conjunction with them one finds an inability to delay, a demand for immediate gratification, and a proclivity to act out under stress. To make matters more difficult, these characteristics are frequently combined with a sense of entitlement.

In the extreme, difficulties in impulse control present themselves as episodes of explosive rage, directed to other people and resulting in bodily injury or even death. Slightly less severe is explosive rage in which inanimate objects are destroyed. Lesser but still obvious problems include childish tantrums and seemingly uncontrolled verbal abuse. More subtle defects include the tendency to excessive drug and alcohol use, uncontrolled gambling, accident proneness, and the tendency to leave work or interpersonal situations under stress.

Problems in impulse control and frustration tolerance are common. They invariably are seen in borderline and psychotic individuals but also occur in many of the lower-level character disorders, in the addictions, and, to a lesser degree, in many of the neuroses.

A-6. How Are Thought Processes Described?

This ego function reflects the ability to think logically, coherently, abstractly, and intelligibly. The term *secondary process thinking* is used to describe goal-directed, logical, and easily understood thinking, typically used by most adults. *Primary process thinking*, most often associated with schizophrenia but also typical of small children and of adult dreams, is a seemingly illogical and idiosyncratic way of thinking, yet has definite rules of its own. Primary process thinking is characterized by condensation, displacement, absence of negatives, absence of qualifiers, timelessness, mutually contradictory coexisting ideas, representation by allusion, and predicative identification. Whereas the normal person accepts identity only on the basis of identical subjects, the paleologician (schizophrenic), invoking the principle of predicative identification, accepts identity based on identical predicates (Arieti, 1995). Thus, if two people are wearing identical shirts, they are assumed to be the same person; if two people or objects have like parts, they are assumed to be identical (pars pro toto).

The term *formal thought disorder* has been used to describe the difficulty in conceptual thinking that occurs when there is an intrusion of primary process thinking where secondary process ought to be. The term *thought disorder* was employed by Bleuler (1950) as characteristic of schizophrenia. For a time it was in vogue to focus on the patient's thinking patterns to see if a formal thought disorder could be demonstrated, thus justifying the diagnosis of schizophrenia.

Several examples of thought disorders involving predicative identification may be useful. A middle-aged Jewish man, upon entering the office, said that he could sing better than Cantor Grazinnitski. When asked how he arrived at this idea, he said that on the way to the office, he passed a girl in a yellow dress. Yellow was the color of butter, and from butter, he went to better, and got the idea that be could sing better than the cantor. The predicates yellow, butter, and better were all equated via the primary process, enabling the patient to reach his conclusion. A second example is that of a young woman who felt that her psychiatrist, whenever he touched his glasses, was giving her signals to trust him. She arrived at this conclusion by noting the rust color of the psychiatrist's glasses and thinking of the term trust.

Psychiatric research (Pope and Lipinski, 1978; Pope, Lipinski, Cohen, Axelrod, 1980; Procci, 1976) has indicated that the thought disorder is not necessarily pathognomonic for schizophrenia, particularly when comparing schizophrenia with bipolar illness. The presence of marked or frequent problems in conceptual thinking, however, is frequently associated with schizophrenia and certainly most often indicates some psychotic process. Brief reversible regressions in conceptual thinking, under stress or in unstructured situations, are generally thought to be characteristic of many borderline patients. Often, the Rorschach test can demonstrate difficulties of this type that are not apparent during the clinical interview.

A-7. What Are Interpersonal Relations and How Do They Differ from Object Relations?

The term *interpersonal relations* is used here to denote the personal interactions that actually take place between individuals, either in the present or in the past. In contrast, the term *object relations* denotes the internalized derivatives of these interactions. Those internalized derivatives include various types of internal objects, including introjects and self and object representations. For our purposes we will focus on self and object representations. Object representations are built up in the ego as the result of the way the individual has perceived, processed, and internalized past interpersonal experiences. Self representations are built up as a result of the way the individual has perceived, processed, and internalized his or her varying past conceptions of himself or herself.. Thus, interpersonal relations describes interactions, involvements, and experiences between individuals; object relations describes a state within the ego.

As we will discuss later, there is some controversy concerning the use of the terms self and object representations. The conceptualization just presented represents one of a number of ways these terms are used. Although a listing of ego functions usually includes the term object relations, what is described sometimes is more in accordance with interpersonal relations. Here, interpersonal relations, although technically not an ego function, will be listed as one ego function, describing the individual's typical relationships with other people. The self and object representations underlying these interpersonal relations will be detailed under a separate ego function, that relating to the representational world.

A mature interpersonal relationship is one in which the individual, in addition to attempting to gratify his or her own needs in the relationship, views the other as a separate person with special needs and desires. Emphasis is placed on helping the other person to gratify these special needs and desires, in addition to gratifying one's own needs. Respect, concern, and empathy are demonstrated in the relationship. There is always the quality of attempting to gratify one's own needs (at least unconsciously) in even the most mature interpersonal relationship.

A lower level of interpersonal relationship, common in borderline and psychotic individuals, is one in which the other person is basically "used" only to gratify one's own needs. Sometimes this kind of interpersonal relation appears more mature on the surface, because the individual, in meeting his or her own needs, may simultaneously gratify the needs of the other person. There is, however, no feeling for the other person as a separate individual with needs, no concern, no empathy, no depth of understanding, and no mutuality. Occasionally, individuals can form long-term relationships based on this more primitive kind of interpersonal relationship. An example is the marriage of a very passive, dependent individual, with a great need to be taken care of to a dominant, parental individual with an equally great need to care for others. Another example is the relationship of a sadist to a masochist.

An even lower level of interpersonal relationship is one in which the individual distorts the characteristics of the other person in accordance with his own needs. Thus, if the need is to be taken care of, the individual acts as if the other is strong and powerful, all evidence to the contrary being discarded. Relationships of this nature typically involve the use of very primitive defenses, along with at least subtle defects in reality testing. A still lower level of interpersonal relationship, basically confined to psychotic individuals, is one in which there is a loss of ego boundaries and a fusion with the other individual.

A-8. What Is the Representational World and How Does It Relate to Self and Object Representations?

The *representational world* is another complex and controversial concept. As noted by Boesky (1983), there is disagreement about the usages of the terms *self representation* and *object representation*. Although self and object representations are listed here as an ego function, there is even disagreement about whether this is the case. Although Sandler and Rosenblatt (1962), Jacobson (1964), and Kernberg (1976), among others, view these mental representations as part of the system ego, Boesky (1983) and others prefer to think of these representations as being formed by the interaction of ego, id, and superego, and not residing in one system alone. Boesky notes theoretical difficulty with integrating the "representational" model with the structural theory. He views this integration as possible but difficult.

Despite these problems, the concepts of the representational world appear with great frequency in the literature, particularly with regard to borderline and psychotic individuals. Viewing self and object representations as part of the system ego simplifies, in a way, the concept of mental representations and seems the most helpful in understanding the literature on the borderline and the psychotic patient.

In the healthy individual, various self representations are gradually built up in the ego, coalesced, integrated, and synthesized into a stable, cohesive, and realistic sense of self. Concomitantly, various object representations are gradually formed in the ego, coalesced, integrated, and synthesized into a stable, cohesive, and realistic sense of other. These self and object representations provide the healthy individual with a stable, integrated identity.

Identity diffusion is a term that Erikson (1956) and Kernberg (1967, 1975) use to describe the lack of an integrated self-concept and the lack of an integrated, stable concept of objects. Kernberg believes identity diffusion to be a core problem of the borderline individual. The individual with identity diffusion has not integrated good self-images (representations) with bad self-images (representations), but, instead, retains multiple, contradictory self-images, some good and some bad. At one time, one self-image is invoked; at another time, a different one. A meaningful, integrated image of the self is never formed. The same pattern occurs with objects. The individual's concept remains only as a series of contradictory object images (representations), some good and some bad, with the attainment of meaningful, comprehensive images of others greatly lacking.

A level of organization somewhat higher than identity diffusion is the representational world often described for the narcissistic personality. Here the self and object representations are stable and cohesive, yet primitive, archaic, and unrealistic, relating to the underlying "grandiose self." Kohut (1971, 1977, 1984) views these archaic self and object representations as related to normally occurring infantile configurations that were never properly integrated. Kernberg (1978), in contrast, sees them as the result of the development of very specific psychopathological structures. He believes that the self and object representations are distorted by a pathological fusion of the ideal self, the ideal object, and the actual self. At a level below identity diffusion is the representational world of the psychotic, characterized by at least an intermittent fusion of self and object representations and a corresponding blurring of reality.

A-9. How Are Defense Mechanisms Conceptualized?

In accordance with classical psychoanalytic theory, defense mechanisms (or defenses) refer to habitually occurring, unconscious mental phenomena employed by the ego to resolve conflict between the instinctual drives, the superego, and external reality. Defenses are developed basically to help hold in check unwanted aggressive or libidinal drives. Typically, an upsurge in aggressive or libidinal drive is opposed initially by the superego. The ego recognizes a danger, signals anxiety, and initiates a defense. Alternatively, one can bypass "drive theory" and think of defenses solely in relation to anxiety. There are an unlimited number of potential defenses, because virtually any mental phenomenon can serve as a defensive function. Various specific defenses, however, have been described and popularized. The most commonly mentioned defenses include repression, regression, reaction formation, undoing, isolation, intellectualization, rationalization, projection, denial, displacement, introjection, turning against the self, and sublimation.

Every individual uses a wide variety of defenses, yet each individual can be characterized as typically using certain specific defenses in day-to-day functioning, and other specific defenses under stress. If these defenses are known, the therapist has invaluable clinical information about the individual.

Everyone uses certain "primitive" defenses early in life. These "primitive" defenses typically evolve into more mature defenses as development proceeds. By early adulthood, a stable pattern of typical defenses has emerged, a pattern that is henceforth very resistant to change. Certain specific defenses have come to be associated not only with specific developmental periods, but also with specific levels of psychopathology. Thus, the broad psychopathological groupings of neurotic, borderline, narcissistic, and psychotic are characterized by different specific defensive patterns. Within these broad groupings, different subgroups have also been characterized by the use of even more specific defenses. A number of hierarchies of defenses have been proposed.

Vaillant (1971) proposes four categories in his hierarchy. The first and lowest level comprises what he calls "narcissistic." Vaillant here uses an outdated definition of "narcissistic"; what he actually is denoting are psychotic defenses. These defenses are thought to be common in healthy individuals before age 5 years, in adult dreams and fantasies, and in psychotic individuals. These defenses tend to alter reality and are very difficult to change by psychotherapy; they include delusional projection, psychotic denial, and distortion. The second level comprises what Vaillant calls "immature" defenses. These defenses are thought to be common in healthy individuals aged 3 to 16 years; among adults they are most often used by those with character disorders and affective disorders. These defenses cause the individual to appear socially undesirable; they are also resistant to change by psychotherapy. In this group, Vaillant includes projection, schizoid fantasy, hypochondriasis, passive-aggressive behavior, and acting out. The third level comprises the "neurotic" defenses. These defenses are thought to be common in healthy individuals aged 3 to 90 years and are characteristic of neurotic disorders. They are the defenses most commonly described in the literature—repression, intellectualization, isolation, rationalization, undoing, ritual, magical thinking, displacement, reaction formation, and dissociation, among others. They are thought to be amenable to change by psychotherapy. The fourth and highest level of defenses consists of the "mature" defenses. These defenses are thought to occur in healthy individuals aged 12 to 90 years and are not commonly thought of as defenses per se. They include altruism, humor, suppression, anticipation, and sublimation.

Absent from Vaillant's hierarchy are what have become known as the "borderline" defenses. These defenses fit into a category between Vaillant's "narcissistic" (psychotic) defenses and his "immature" defenses. They include splitting, primitive idealization, projective identification, primitive denial, omnipotence, and devaluation. In addition to these "borderline" defenses, one can add several "narcissistic" (psychotic) defenses to Vaillant's list: hallucinations, fusion, fragmentation, and dedifferentiation. With these modifications, Vaillant's hierarchy of defenses can be of great value.

Several generalizations about this defensive hierarchy are relevant. Individuals do have the tendency to use certain broad categories of defenses, but these patterns are not completely consistent. It is important to classify the individual's usual defensive pattern, both in day-to-day situations and under stress. In usual daily functioning, the typical psychotic does not use predominantly psychotic defenses, nor does the typical borderline individual use predominantly borderline defenses. Better generalizations, although they are only generalizations, are as follows. A typical psychotic uses some combination of neurotic, immature, borderline, and sometimes psychotic defenses in day-to-day functioning but shows a tendency to use psychotic defenses under stress. A typical borderline individual uses mature, neurotic, immature, and borderline defenses in day-to-day functioning, displaying a proclivity for the borderline and, occasionally, psychotic defenses under stress. In contrast, a typical neurotic uses mainly neurotic and mature defenses in day-to-day functioning, accentuating certain specific neurotic defenses under stress and occasionally using immature and borderline defenses.

A-10. What Other Ego Functions Might We Consider?

There are several other ego functions that are worth considering. The descriptions of these ego functions are basically those of Bellak (Bellak 1970; Bellak and Meyers, 1975).

Judgment

Judgment refers to the ability, first, to be aware of the likely consequences of intended or actual behavior, and second, to act in accordance with this awareness. This ego function is a complex one, clearly related to three ego functions already discussed—reality testing, impulse control and frustration tolerance, and thought processes. Isolated difficulties in judgment are common. More global difficulties are often associated with both borderline and psychotic conditions.

Adaptive Regression in the Service of the Ego

This ego function was first described by Kris (1952), who originally used the term to characterize creativity. Adaptive regression in the service of the ego (ARISE) contains three components. The first involves the ability to suspend secondary process thinking and to allow more primitive and unconscious forms of ideation to emerge. This is the regression. The second component involves the capacity to reverse the regression readily and to return to secondary process thinking. The third component involves the capacity to use the regression for adaptive and creative ends. In addition to its clear relationship to creativity, ARISE is necessary for the pursuit of intensive psychotherapy. Typically, obsessive-compulsive individuals display difficulty in enacting the first component, regression. Psychotic and borderline individuals, in contrast, have no difficulty regressing. The problem with these individuals is in the last two components—reversing the regression and using it adaptively and creatively.

Stimulus Barrier

This ego function has two components. The first component—the receptive one—refers to the individual's sensitivity to and awareness of sensory stimulation, both internal and external. The second component— the expressive one—reflects the individual's ability to cope with various kinds and levels of stimulation. Individuals who are either oversensitive to stimulation or have difficulty in coping with this stimulation present special problems. Insomnia, easy distractibility, and difficulty in concentrating are examples of mild difficulties regarding the stimulus barrier. More severe difficulties include disorganization and loss of control in response to overstimulation. Problems with the stimulus barrier are frequent in patients with difficulties of organic origin. Certain theoretical conceptualizations of schizophrenia (Grotstein, 1977a, 1977b) have focused on defects in this ego function.

Autonomous Functions

These ego functions have been described extensively by Hartmann (1939, 1955). The term *autonomy* basically means freedom from conflict. Primary autonomous functions are those functions with which an individual is born that typically do not become involved in conflict. These include, among others, orientation, memory, perception, attention, intelligence, language, sensation, and motor expression. Defects in the primary autonomous functions are most often indicative of organicity. Secondary autonomous functions are behavior patterns and traits that, although they develop out of conflict, later become free from conflict. Although these secondary autonomous functions can sometimes become reinvolved in conflict, they most often remain stable.

Synthesis Integration

Basically, this ego function represents the way the individual integrates all the other ego functions into a coherent and smoothly operating whole. It is a complex ego function, difficult to measure. The synthetic-integrative function can be described in terms of two components. The first component involves the ability to integrate potentially contradictory experiences or ideas. These include such terms as self and object representations, affects, thoughts, feelings, and actions. The second component involves the ability to integrate experiences or ideas that are not contradictory. Both borderline and psychotic individuals show impairments in this function.

REFERENCES

Adler, G. (1985). *Borderline psychopathology and its treatment*. New York: Jason Aronson, Inc.

American Psychiatric Association. (1994). *Diagnostic and statistical manual of mental disorders* (4th ed.). Washington, DC: Author.

Arieti, S. (1955). *Interpretation of schizophrenia*. New York: Robert Brunner.

Arlow, J. (1985). Interpretation and psychoanalytic psychotherapy: A clinical illustration. In E. A. Schwaber (Ed.), *The transference in psychotherapy* (pp. 103–120). New York: International Universities Press.

Arlow, J., & Brenner, C. (1964). *Psychoanalytic concepts and the structural theory*. New York: International Universities Press.

Arlow, J., & Brenner, C. (1969). The psychopathology of the psychoses: A proposed revision. *International Journal of Psycho-Analysis, 50*, 5–14.

Arlow, J., & Brenner, C. (1990). The psychoanalytic process. *Psychoanalytic Quarterly, 59*, 678–692.

Aron, L. (1996). *A meeting of minds: Mutuality in psychoanalysis*. Hillsdale, NJ: The Analytic Press.

Atwood, G., & Stolorow, R. (1984). *Structures of subjectivity: Explorations in psychoanalytic phenomenology*. Hillsdale, NJ: The Analytic Press.

Bacal, H. (Ed.). (1998). *Optimal responsiveness: How therapists heal their patients*. Northvale, NJ: Jason Aronson, Inc.

Bak, R. (1970). Recent developments in psychoanalysis: A critical summary of the main theme of the 26th International Psycho-Analytical Congress in Rome. *International Journal of Psycho-Analysis, 51*, 255–264.

Balint, M. (1968). *The basic fault*. London: Tavistock.

Beck, A. (1976). *Cognitive therapy and the emotional disorders*. New York: International Universities Press.

Bellak, L. (1958). *Schizophrenia: A review of the syndrome*. New York: Logos Press.

Bellak, L. (1970). Recent developments in psychoanalysis: A critical summary of the main theme of the 26th International Psycho-Analytical Congress in Rome. *International Journal of Psychoanalysis, 51*, 255–264.

Bellak, L. (1970). The validity and usefulness of the concept of the schizophrenic syndrome. In B. Cancro (Ed.), *The schizophrenic reaction* (pp. 41–58). New York: Brunner/ Mazel.

Bellak, L., & Meyers, B. (1975). Ego function assessment and analysability. *International Review of Psychoanalysis, 2*, 413–427.

Benjamin, J. (1990). Recognition and destruction: An outline of intersubjectivity. *Psychoanalytic Psychology, 7*(Suppl.), 33–47.

Beres, D. (1956). Ego deviation and the concept of schizophrenia. In *Psychoanalytic study of the child* (Vol. 2). New York: International Universities Press.

Bibring, E. (1954). Psychoanalysis and the dynamic psychotherapies. *Journal of the American Psychoanalytic Association, 2,* 745–770.

Bion, W. (1967). *Second thoughts: Selected papers on psychoanalysis.* New York: Basic Books.

Bleuler, E. (1950). *Dementia Praecox or the Group of Schizophrenia* (German, 1911). New York: International Universities Press.

Boesky, D. (1983). The problem of mental representation in self and object theory. *Psychoanalytic Quarterly, 52,* 564–583.

Brenner, C. (1982). *The mind in conflict.* New York: International Universities Press.

Brenner, C. (1994). The mind as conflict and compromise formation. *Journal of Clinical Psychoanalysis, 3:* 473–488.

Busch, F. (1999). *Rethinking clinical technique.* Northvale, NJ: Jason Aronson, Inc.

Chused, J. (1991). The evocative power of enactments. *Journal of the American Psychoanalytic Association, 39,* 615–639.

Erikson, E. (1956). The problem of ego identity. *Journal of the American Psychoanalytic Association, 4,* 56–121.

Fairbairn, W. R. (1954). *An object-relations theory of the personality.* New York: Basic Books.

Federn, P. (1952). *Ego psychology and the psychoses.* New York: Basic Books.

Ferenczi, S. (1932). *The clinical diary of Sandor Ferenczi.* Cambridge, MA: Harvard University Press.

Freeman, T. (1970). The psychopathology of the psychoses: A reply to Arlow and Brenner. *International Journal of Psycho-Analysis, 51,* 407–415.

Freud, A. (1936). *The ego and the mechanisms of defense.* New York: International Universities Press.

Freud, S. (1923). The ego and the id. *Standard Edition, 19,* 3–66. London: The Hogarth Press.

Freud, S. (1926). Inhibitions, symptoms, and anxiety. *Standard Edition, 20,* 75–174.

Freud, S. (1936). *The ego and the mechanisms of defense.* New York: International Universities Press.

Freud, S. (1940). An outline of psychoanalysis. *Standard Edition, 23,* 144–207. London: The Hogarth Press.

Gabbard, G. O., & Wilkinson, S. (1994). *Management of countertransference with borderline patients.* Washington, DC: American Psychiatric Press.

Gill, M. (1954). Psychoanalysis and exploratory psychotherapy. *Journal of the American Psychoanalytic Association, 2,* 771–797.

Goldberg, A. (1988). *A fresh look at psychoanalysis: A view from self psychology.* Hillsdale, NJ: The Analytic Press.

Goldberg, A. (1990). *The prison house of psychoanalysis.* Hillsdale, NJ: The Analytic Press.

Goldstein, W. (1985). *An introduction to the borderline conditions.* Northvale, NJ: Jason Aronson, Inc.

Goldstein, W. (1991). Clarification of projective identification. *American Journal of Psychiatry, 148,* 153–161.

Goldstein, W. (1996). *Dynamic psychotherapy with the borderline patient.* Northvale, NJ: Jason Aronson, Inc.

Gray, P. (1994). *The ego and analysis of defense.* Northvale, NJ: Jason Aronson, Inc.

Greenberg, J., & Mitchell, S. (1983). *Object relations in psychoanalytic theory.* Cambridge, MA: Harvard University Press.

Grotstein, J. (1977a). The psychoanalytic concept of schizophrenia. I. The dilemma. *International Journal of Psychoanalysis, 58,* 403–425.

Grotstein, J. (1977b). The psychoanalytic concept of schizophrenia. II. Reconciliation. *International Journal of Psychoanalysis, 58,* 427–452.

Guntrip, H. (1961). *Personality structure and human interaction.* London: Hogarth Press.

Hamilton, G. (1988). *Self and others: Object relations theory in practice.* Northvale, NJ: Jason Aronson, Inc.

Hartmann, H. (1939). *Ego psychology and the problem of adaptation.* New York: International Universities Press.

Hartmann, H. (1955). Notes on the theory of sublimation. *Journal of the American Psychoanalytic Association, 10,* 9–29.

Hoffman, I. (1983). The patient as interpreter of the analyst's experience. *Contemporary Psychoanalysis, 19,* 389–422.

Hoffman, I. (1996). The intimate and ironic authority of the psychoanalyst's presence. *Psychoanalytic Quarterly, 65,* 102–136.

Horner, A. (1991). *Psychoanalytic object relations therapy.* Northvale, NJ: Jason Aronson, Inc.

Jacobson, E. (1964). *The self and the object world.* New York: International Universities Press.

Kernberg, O. (1967). Borderline personality organization. *Journal of the American Psychoanalytic Association, 15,* 641–685.

Kernberg, O. (1975). *Borderline conditions and pathological narcissism.* New York: Jason Aronson, Inc.

Kernberg, O. (1976). *Object relations theory and clinical psychoanalysis.* New York: Jason Aronson, Inc.

Kernberg, O. (1978). Contrasting approaches to the psychotherapy of borderline conditions. In J. F. Masterson (Ed.), *New perspectives of psychotherapy of the borderline adult* (pp. 77–104). New York: Brunner/Mazel.

Kernberg, O. (1980). *Internal world and external reality.* New York: Jason Aronson, Inc.

Kernberg, O. (1984). *Severe personality disorders.* New Haven, CT: Yale University Press.

Kernberg, O. (1993). Suicidal behavior in borderline patients: Diagnosis and psychotherapeutic considerations. *American Journal of Psychotherapy, 47,* 245–254.

Kernberg, O., Seltzer, M., Koenigsberg, H., Carr, A., & Appelbaum, A. (1989). *Psychodynamic psychotherapy of borderline patients.* New York: Basic Books.

Kohut, H. (1971). *The analysis of the self.* New York: International Universities Press.

Kohut, H. (1977). *The restoration of the self.* New York: International Universities Press.

Kohut, H. (1984). *How does analysis cure?* Chicago: University of Chicago Press.

Kris, E. (1952). *Psychoanalytic explorations in art.* New York: International Universities Press.

Lichtenberg, J. (1989). *Psychoanalysis and motivation.* Hillsdale, NJ: Analytic Press.

Lichtenberg, J., Lachmann, F., & Fosshage, J. (1992). *Self and motivational systems: Toward a theory of psychoanalytic technique.* Hillsdale, NJ: Analytic Press.

Lichtenberg, J., Lachmann, F., & Fosshage, J. (1996). *The clinical exchange: Techniques derived from self and motivational systems.* Hillsdale, NJ: Analytic Press.

Mahler, M. S., Pine, F., & Bergman, A. (1975). *The psychological birth of the human infant.* New York: Basic Books.

Meissner, W. (1980). A note on projective identification. *Journal of the American Psychoanalytic Association, 28,* 43–67.

Meissner, W. (1988). *Treatment of patients in the borderline spectrum.* Northvale, NJ: Jason Aronson, Inc.

Natterson, J., & Friedman, R. (1995). *A primer of clinical intersubjectivity.* Northvale, NJ: Jason Aronson, Inc.

Pope, H., & Lipinski, J. (1978). Diagnosis in schizophrenia and manic depressive illness. *Archives of General Psychiatry, 35,* 811.

Pope, H., Lipinski, J., Cohen, B., Axelrod, D. (1980). Schizophrenia disorder: An invalid diagnosis? A comparison of schizoaffective disorder, schizophrenia, and affective disorders. *American Journal of Psychiatry, 137,* 921.

Pray, M. (1996). Two different methods of analyzing defense. In M. A. Goldberger (Ed.), *Danger and defense* (53–106). Northvale, NJ: Jason Aronson, Inc.

Procci, W. (1976). Schizo-affective psychosis: Fact or fiction? *Archives of General Psychiatry, 33,* 1167.

Renik, O. (1996). The perils of neutrality. *Psychoanalytic Quarterly, 65,* 495–517.

Renik, O. (1999). Playing one's cards face up in analysis: An approach to the problem of self disclosure. *Psychoanalytic Quarterly, 68,* 521–539.

Rockland, L. (1992). *Supportive therapy for borderline patients: A psychodynamic approach.* New York: Guilford Press.

Sandler, J., & Rosenblatt, B. (1962). The concept of the representational world. *Psychoanalytic Study of the Child, 17,* 128–145.

Schaffer, N. (1986). The borderline patient and affirmative interpretation. *Bulletin of the Menninger Clinic, 50,* 148–162.

Schuyler, D. (1991). *A practical guide to cognitive therapy.* New York: Norton.

Segal, H. (1981). *The work of Melanie Klein.* New York: Jason Aronson, Inc.

Shane, M., Shane, E., & Gales, M. (1997). *Intimate attachments toward a new self psychology.* New York: Guilford Press.

Stern, D. (1985). *The interpersonal world of the infant.* New York: Basic Books.

Stolorow, R., Brandschaft, B., & Atwood, G. (1987). *Psychoanalytic treatment: An intersubjective approach.* Hillsdale, NJ: Analytic Press.

Teicholz, J. (1999). *Kohut, Loewald, and the postmoderns.* Hillsdale, NJ: Analytic Press.

Ticho, E. (1970). Differences between psychoanalysis and psychotherapy. *Bulletin of the Menninger Clinic, 34,* 128–139.

Vaillant, G. (1971). Theoretical hierarchy of adaptive ego mechanisms. *Psychiatry, 24,* 107–118.

Winnicott, D. W. (1958). *Collected papers: Through paediatrics to psychoanalysis.* New York: Basic Books.

Winnicott, D. (1958). Primary maternal preoccupation. In *Collected papers: Through pediatrics to psychoanalysis* (pp. 306–315). New York: Basic Books.

Winnicott, D. (1965). The theory of the parent-infant relationship. In *The maturational processes and the facilitating environment* (pp. 37–55). New York: International Universities Press.

Wolf, E. (1988). *Treating the self.* New York: Guilford Press.

Yeomans, E., Seizer, M., & Clarin, J. (1992). *Treating the borderline patient: contract-based approach.* New York: Basic Books.

INDEX

127